CRIMINAL JUSTICE, LAW ENFORCEMENT
AND CORRECTIONS SERIES

ORGANIZED CRIME IN THE U. S.

Criminal Justice, Law Enforcement and Corrections Series

Gun Ownership and the Second Amendment
Pjeter D. Baldrige
2009. ISBN: 978-1-60692-226-2

Homicide Investigations
Allan B. Smythe
2009. ISBN: 978-1-60692-258-3

Digital Surveillance: Laws, Security and Related Issues
Joseph G. Massingale (Editor)
2009. ISBN: 978-1-60692-312-2

Mass Incarceration and Offender Reentry in the United States
Russell D. Javitze (Editor)
2009. ISBN: 978-1-60692-657-4

Incarceration and the Family: Issues, Effects and Approaches to Successful Reentry
United States Department of Health and Human Services
2009. ISBN: 978-1-60692-933-9

Batterer Intervention: Program Approaches and Criminal Justice Strategies
Kerry Healey, Christine Smith, and Chris O'Sullivan
2009. ISBN: 978-1-60692-934-6
(Hardcover)

Batterer Intervention: Program Approaches and Criminal Justice Strategies
Kerry Healey, Christine Smith and Chris O'Sullivan
2009. ISBN: 978-1-60876-537-9
(Online Book)

Delinquency: Causes, Reduction and Prevention
Ozan Sahin and Joseph Maier (Editor)
2009. ISBN: 978-1-60741-558-9

Homicide: Trends, Causes and Prevention
Randal B. Toliver and Ulrich R. Coyne (Editors)
2009. ISBN: 978-1-60741-625-8

Violent Crime and Prisons: Population, Health Conditions and Recidivism
Aidan Renshaw and Emelina Suárez (Editors)
2009. ISBN: 978-1-60741-668-5

Policing the Police: Knowledge Management in Law Enforcement
Petter Gottschalk
2009. ISBN: 978-1-60741-765-1
(Hardcover)

Policing the Police: Knowledge Management in Law Enforcement
Petter Gottschalk
2009. ISBN: 978-1-60876-653-6
(Online Book)

Selective Prosecution in the Federal Criminal Justice System?
Kevin H. Mabe (Editor)
2010. ISBN: 978-1-60692-684-0

Police and Augmented Reality Technology
Matthew D. Blount (Editor)
2010. ISBN: 978-1-60692-206-4

Guidelines for Domestic FBI Operations
Carlo Bianchi (Editor)
2010. ISBN: 978-1-60692-798-4

Revisiting the Social Contract: Community Justice and Public Safety
Kathleen Auerhahn and Caitlin J. McGuire
2010. ISBN: 978-1-60876-446-4
(Softcover)

Mass Marketing and Consumer Fraud: Background, Issues and Data
Martin A. Parham (Editor)
2010. ISBN: 978-1-60692-793-9

Organized Crime in the U.S.
Wesley B. Knowles (Editor)
2010. ISBN: 978-1-60741-524-4

CRIMINAL JUSTICE, LAW ENFORCEMENT
AND CORRECTIONS SERIES

ORGANIZED CRIME IN THE U. S.

WESLEY B. KNOWLES
EDITOR

Nova Science Publishers, Inc.
New York

For permission to use material from this book please contact us:
Telephone 631-231-7269; Fax 631-231-8175
Web Site: http://www.novapublishers.com

LIBRARY OF CONGRESS CATALOGING-IN-PUBLICATION DATA

>Organized crime in the U.S. / editor, Wesley B. Knowles.
> p. cm.
> Includes index.
> ISBN 978-1-60741-524-4 (hardcover)
> 1. Organized crime--United States. 2. Alien criminals--United
>States. I. Knowles, Wesley B.
> HV6446.O743 2009
> 364.1060973--dc22

2009035597

Published by Nova Science Publishers, Inc. ✈ New York

CONTENTS

PREFACE

Organized crime has taken on an increasingly transnational nature, and with more open borders and the expansion of the Internet, criminals endanger the United States not only from within the borders, but beyond. Threats come from a variety of criminal organizations, including Russian, Asian, Italian, Balkan, Middle Eastern, and African syndicates. Policymakers may question whether the tools they have provided the federal government to combat organized crime are still effective for countering today's evolving risks. In the wake of the economic downturn, organized crime could further weaken the economy with illegal activities (such as cigarette trafficking and tax evasion scams) that result in a loss of tax revenue for state and federal governments. On the national security front, experts and policymakers have expressed concern over a possible nexus between organized crime and terrorism. Despite the difference in motivation for organized crime (profit) and terrorism (ideology), the linking element of the two is money. This book consists of public documents which have been located, gathered, combined, reformatted, and enhanced with a subject index, selectively edited and bound to provide easy access.

Chapter 1 - Organized crime threatens multiple facets of the United States, including the economy and national security. In fact, the Organized Crime Council was recently reconvened for the first time in 15 years to address this continued threat. Organized crime has taken on an increasingly transnational nature, and with more open borders and the expansion of the Internet, criminals endanger the United States not only from within the borders, but beyond. Threats come from a variety of criminal organizations, including Russian, Asian, Italian, Balkan, Middle Eastern, and African syndicates. Policymakers may question whether the tools they have provided the federal government to combat organized crime are still effective for countering today's evolving risks.

In the wake of the economic downturn, organized crime could further weaken the economy with illegal activities (such as cigarette trafficking and tax evasion scams) that result in a loss of tax revenue for state and federal governments. Fraudulent activities in domains such as strategic commodities, credit, insurance, stocks, securities and investments could further weaken the already-troubled financial market.

On the national security front, experts and policymakers have expressed concern over a possible nexus between organized crime and terrorism. Despite the difference in motivation for organized crime (profit) and terrorism (ideology), the linking element for the two is money. Terrorists may potentially obtain funding for their operations from partnering directly with organized crime groups or modeling their profitable criminal acts. Even if organized crime groups and terrorist organizations do not form long-term alliances, the possibility of short-term business alliances may be of concern to policymakers.

In light of these developments, several possible issues for Congress arise. One issue centers on whether the evolving nature of organized crime requires new enforcement tools. Some policymakers have suggested that current laws may not be effective at countering present threats from organized crime. As organized criminals threaten American society from both within and outside U.S. borders, should Congress expand law enforcement's extraterritorial jurisdiction to investigate and prosecute these criminals, and to what extent should Congress encourage multilateral—both domestic and international—crime fighting efforts? Legislation has been introduced in the 111th Congress (H.R. 1793, S. 49, S. 378, and S. 386, for example) that would expand the list of predicate offenses under the Racketeer Influenced and Corrupt Organizations Act (RICO), clarify the definition of money laundering, and expand the international money laundering statute.

Another possible issue for Congress concerns whether the resources that the federal government allocates to organized crime matters are adequate and appropriately allocated to counter the threats it poses. Following the terrorist attacks of September 11, 2001, national priorities and federal resources shifted away from more traditional crime fighting—including that of organized crime—toward counterterrorism and counterintelligence. For instance, the number of federal agents actually working on organized crime matters and the number of organized crime cases opened in FY2004 decreased relative to levels before September 11, 2001. This report will be updated as needed.

Chapter 2 - By the late 20th century, organized criminal groups throughout the world were able to exploit the same economic liberalization, technology advances, and open borders that enabled multinational corporations to grow and prosper. Today, organized crime is a transnational phenomenon—and a cause for worldwide concern.

Transnational crime groups may have profited more from globalization than legitimate businesses, which are subject to domestic and host country laws and regulations. Transnational crime syndicates and networks, abetted by official corruption, blackmail, and intimidation, can use open markets and open societies to their full advantage.

As part of its effort to build an international research agenda that will help the United States better understand potential threats from transnational crime, the National Institute of Justice (NIJ) supported a project to preliminarily assess organized crime in eight Asian countries or administrative regions (Cambodia, China, Hong Kong, Japan, Macau, the Philippines, Taiwan, and Thailand); pinpoint research issues of mutual interest to U.S. and Asian researchers; identify potential research partners (and their affiliated institutions) in Asia who might work collaboratively on these issues; and locate indigenous data sources that would be accessible to U.S. investigators.

Chapters 3 through Chapters 8 feature information about regional organized crime taken from the Federal Bureau of Investigation's web site. African criminal enterprises have developed quickly since the 1980s due to the globalization of the world's economies and the great advances in communications technology. Easier international travel, expanded world trade, and financial transactions that cross national borders have enabled them to branch out of local and regional crime to target international victims and develop criminal networks within more prosperous countries and regions.

In: Organized Crime in the U.S.
Editor: Wesley B. Knowles

ISBN: 978-1-60741-524-4

Chapter 1

ORGANIZED CRIME IN THE UNITED STATES: TRENDS AND ISSUES FOR CONGRESS

Kristin M. Finklea

SUMMARY

Organized crime threatens multiple facets of the United States, including the economy and national security. In fact, the Organized Crime Council was recently reconvened for the first time in 15 years to address this continued threat. Organized crime has taken on an increasingly transnational nature, and with more open borders and the expansion of the Internet, criminals endanger the United States not only from within the borders, but beyond. Threats come from a variety of criminal organizations, including Russian, Asian, Italian, Balkan, Middle Eastern, and African syndicates. Policymakers may question whether the tools they have provided the federal government to combat organized crime are still effective for countering today's evolving risks.

In the wake of the economic downturn, organized crime could further weaken the economy with illegal activities (such as cigarette trafficking and tax evasion scams) that result in a loss of tax revenue for state and federal governments. Fraudulent activities in domains such as strategic commodities, credit, insurance, stocks, securities and investments could further weaken the already-troubled financial market.

On the national security front, experts and policymakers have expressed concern over a possible nexus between organized crime and terrorism. Despite the difference in motivation for organized crime (profit) and terrorism (ideology), the linking element for the two is money. Terrorists may potentially obtain funding for their operations from partnering directly with organized crime groups or modeling their profitable criminal acts. Even if organized crime groups and terrorist organizations do not form long-term alliances, the possibility of short-term business alliances may be of concern to policymakers.

In light of these developments, several possible issues for Congress arise. One issue centers on whether the evolving nature of organized crime requires new enforcement tools. Some policymakers have suggested that current laws may not be effective at countering present threats from organized crime. As organized criminals threaten American society from both within and outside U.S. borders, should Congress expand law enforcement's extraterritorial jurisdiction to investigate and prosecute these criminals, and to what extent should Congress encourage multilateral—both domestic and international—crime fighting efforts? Legislation has been introduced in the 111th Congress (H.R. 1793, S. 49, S. 378, and S. 386, for example) that would expand the list of predicate offenses under the Racketeer Influenced and Corrupt Organizations Act (RICO), clarify the definition of money laundering, and expand the international money laundering statute.

Another possible issue for Congress concerns whether the resources that the federal government allocates to organized crime matters are adequate and appropriately allocated to counter the threats it poses. Following the terrorist attacks of September 11, 2001, national priorities and federal resources shifted away from more traditional crime fighting—including that of organized crime—toward counterterrorism and counterintelligence. For instance, the number of federal agents actually working on organized crime matters and the number of organized crime cases opened in FY2004 decreased relative to levels before September 11, 2001. This report will be updated as needed.

INTRODUCTION

Organized crime threatens the economy, national security, and other interests of the United States.[1] Particularly in the past several decades, organized crime has been evolving and taking on an increasingly transnational nature. With more open borders and the expansion of the Internet, organized criminals threaten the United States not only from within the borders, but beyond. Organized crime stretches far beyond the Italian mafia, encompassing

Russian, Asian, Balkan, Middle Eastern, and African syndicates. Even though organized crime has not received as much recent media or congressional attention as have other national concerns, such as the threat of terrorism, these criminals have not ceased their illicit activities.

Illustrating that the threats from organized crime remain, former Attorney General Michael Mukasey reconvened the Organized Crime Council (OCC) in April 2008 to address the evolving threats from organized crime.[2] Beyond the individual illegal activities committed by organized crime groups (e.g., gambling, prostitution, labor racketeering, smuggling/trafficking, extortion, theft, murder, and money laundering), the OCC has indicated that these organizations may

- penetrate the energy and other strategic sectors of the economy;
- provide logistical and other support to terrorists, foreign intelligence services, and governments;
- smuggle/traffic people and contraband goods into the United States;
- exploit the United States and international financial system to move illicit funds;
- use cyberspace to target U.S. victims and infrastructure;
- manipulate securities exchanges and perpetrate sophisticated frauds;
- corrupt or seek to corrupt public officials in the United States and abroad; and
- use violence or the threat of violence as a basis for power.

The domestic impact from the activities of organized crime groups thus extends beyond what many may consider to be traditional organized crime activities. Congress may wish to consider the impact of organized crime on domestic issues of immediate concern, such as the economy and national security. Do these evolving threats from organized crime require new tools to combat it?

Another issue that the 111th Congress may wish to consider is the adequacy of the resources the federal government allocates to organized crime. Following the terrorist attacks of September 11, 2001, national priorities and federal resources shifted away from more traditional crime fighting—including that of organized crime—toward counterterrorism and counterintelligence. Subsequently, there has been a decrease in the federal law enforcement resources dedicated to organized crime matters and a decrease in the number of federal organized crime cases opened.[3]

Consequently, the policy question facing Congress is, Are the resources that the federal government allocates to organized crime matters sufficient to counter the threats that organized crime pose?

This report provides a background on organized crime in the United States as well as the tools that Congress has afforded for the federal government to combat it. It outlines the trends in federal efforts to investigate and prosecute organized crime. The report then discusses the evolving nature of organized crime, including the domestic impact of organized crime, prominent organized crime groups, and their illegal activities affecting the United States. It concludes with a discussion of issues that the 111th Congress may wish to consider, including the attention the federal government allocates to organized crime matters, the multilateral efforts to combat organized crime, and issues surrounding a potential nexus between organized crime and terrorism.

DEFINITIONS OF ORGANIZED CRIME

A clear definition of organized crime is important for both legal and policy purposes. Some experts suggest that although organized crime is difficult to define, the various attributes of criminal organizations are central to the definition. This report uses the attributes of a criminal organization, in combination with the definitions of organized crime, enterprise, and racketeering as outlined in the current law, as a framework for discussing the trends in organized crime and policy issues for Congress to consider.

Specifically, attributes of organized crime may involve

- structure,
- restricted membership,
- continuity,
- violence or the threat of violence,
- illegal enterprises,
- legitimate business penetration,
- corruption, and
- lack of ideology.[4]

The structure of modern organized crime groups often does not exhibit the rigid hierarchy of more traditional organized crime groups such as the Italian Mafia.[5] Moreover, organized crime groups restrict membership based on a number of factors, including race, ethnicity, kinship, and criminal background.

These criminal organizations continue, even if leadership or membership changes over time. Further, violence and/or the threat of violence are integral aspects of organized crime. Organized crime groups profit from illegal enterprises as well as from infiltrating legitimate businesses. They may attempt to corrupt public officials in order to escape investigation, prosecution, or punishment. Notably, the primary goal of organized crime groups is to make money; these groups are profit-driven rather than ideology-driven (a key distinction between organized crime and terrorist groups).[6]

Statutory Definition

The statutory definition of organized crime stems from the Omnibus Crime Control and Safe Streets Act of 1968, as amended (P.L. 90-351). Current law defines organized crime as "the unlawful activities of the members of a highly organized, disciplined association engaged in supplying illegal goods and services, including but not limited to gambling, prostitution, loan sharking, narcotics, labor racketeering, and other unlawful activities of members of such organizations." This definition describes organized crime in terms of the illegal activities rather than in terms of what constitutes a criminal organization. In the Organized Crime Control Act of 1970 (P.L. 91-452), and more specifically within Title IX—the Racketeer Influenced and Corrupt Organizations Act (RICO)[7]—organized crime is defined in terms of an "enterprise" and a "pattern of racketeering activity."[8] The predicate offenses for racketeering include a host of state and federal crimes listed in 18 U.S.C. § 1961. Although RICO provides a definition for an "enterprise," it does not describe the attributes of a criminal enterprise that distinguish it from a legal enterprise. In addition, this definition describes organized crime more in terms of the illegal activities than in terms of the criminal organization.

Background

Organized crime in the United States has a long-standing history. Although this history has its origins prior to the 20th century, organized crime flourished around the time of Prohibition[9] and grabbed the attention of policymakers. Through most of the 20th century, U. S. law enforcement combated what most consider "traditional" organized crime networks operating inside the United States, including the Italian Mafia, Russian Mafia, Japanese Yakuza, and Chinese Tongs. These criminal organizations were involved in a variety of illegal activities, and in the 1950s and 1 960s, the most profitable of these activities was gambling, followed by loan sharking, narcotics trafficking, extortion, prostitution, bootlegging, and fraud.[10] Other prominent activities of organized crime groups were racketeering, theft, murder, and money laundering.

The national focus on organized crime led to several efforts aimed at investigating and controlling it. These initial efforts included the Senate Special Committee to Investigate Organized Crime in Interstate Commerce in 1950 and 1951 led by Senator Kefauver, Senate hearings on organized crime in 1958 and 1963 led by Senator McClellan,[11] a series of conferences on organized crime at Oyster Bay in 1965 and 1966, and the creation of the 1967 Task Force on Organized Crime. This 1967 Task Force reported that law enforcement measures to curb organized crime had not been successful[12] and, further, that organized crime in America was on the rise.[13] Statistics showed that from 1961 to 1966, the number of individuals indicted by the Organized Crime and Racketeering Section (OCRS) of the Department of Justice (DOJ) rose from 121 to 1,198. Further, the number of those indicted individuals actually convicted rose from 73 to 477.[14] Although the raw number of indictments and convictions rose between 1961 and 1966, CRS analysis revealed that the proportion of individuals from organized crime groups who were convicted during this period actually declined, from 60.3% to 39.8%.[15]

Combating organized crime had been a responsibility primarily of state and local law enforcement.[16] As the scope of organized crime was continuing to increase, Congress recognized the need for better crime fighting tools and the need to further the federal government's role in fighting and prosecuting organized crime.[17]

Omnibus Crime Control and Safe Streets Act

One of the first steps taken by Congress to increase the federal government's role in combating organized crime included a series of congressional hearings in 1967 and 1968 and the enactment of the Omnibus Crime Control and Safe Streets Act of 1968 (P.L. 90-351). The Omnibus Crime Control and Safe Streets Act of 1968 was one of the first major pieces of legislation to directly address organized crime. Specifically, it provided grant money via the Law Enforcement Assistance Administration (LEAA)[18] to state law enforcement agencies to combat organized crime. Included in the Act was the congressional finding that

> organized criminals make extensive use of wire and oral communications in their criminal activities. The interception of such communications to obtain evidence of the commission of crimes or to prevent their commission is an indispensable aid to law enforcement and the administration of justice.

Title III of this Act permitted federal law enforcement agencies to wiretap conversations of suspected criminals, including suspects of organized crime.[19] Electronic wiretapping authority granted in the Omnibus Crime Control and Safe Streets Act of 1968 immediately provided American law enforcement and policymakers with an indication of organized criminals' activity, specifically their involvement in illegally importing and distributing narcotics.[20] Despite these tools to combat criminals, the federal government still lacked the tools to combat criminal organizations.[21]

The Organized Crime Control Act and RICO

The Organized Crime Control Act of 1970 (P.L. 91-452) strengthened the ability of the federal government to combat and prosecute criminal organizations. It provided for Special Grand Juries to investigate multi jurisdictional organized crime; these grand juries are able to produce reports outlining public corruption and organized crime conditions in their respective districts. The Act also allowed for witnesses of organized crime to be granted immunity from prosecution in exchange for testimony. Further, it authorized security for government witnesses or potential witnesses in organized crime cases. This measure laid the groundwork for the Witness Security Program (WITSEC).[22] The WITSEC program allows for the protection and relocation of witnesses and their families, whose lives may be in danger as a result of their testimony in organized and other major crime cases.

Title IX of the Organized Crime Control Act of 1970 created the Racketeer Influenced and Corrupt Organizations Act (RICO).[23] Many view RICO as the single most important piece of organized crime legislation enacted.[24] RICO allows for the prosecution of anyone who participates or conspires to participate in a criminal enterprise/organization through two acts of "racketeering activity" within a 10-year period of time. The predicate offenses for racketeering include various state and federal crimes listed in the U.S. Code.[25] Since its enactment, RICO has been one of the dominant tools used in organized crime prosecutions.

Asset Forfeiture and Money Laundering Statutes

Since the passage of RICO, Congress has enacted legislation regarding asset forfeiture and money laundering, both of which have increased the federal government's ability to combat organized crime.[26] The asset forfeiture and money laundering statutes have provided a means for the federal government to further attack the financial structure and assets of organized crime groups.[27] Although RICO included provisions for asset forfeiture, the Comprehensive Crime Control Act of 1984 (P.L. 98-473) expanded upon these provisions. Specifically, Title II of Chapter III—the Comprehensive Forfeiture Act of 1984—amended RICO by specifying that proceeds (both tangible and intangible) obtained directly or indirectly from racketeering activity were subject to forfeiture. This Act also established the Department of Justice's Asset Forfeiture Fund in the Department of the Treasury. The rules for civil forfeiture proceedings were later revised in the Civil Asset Forfeiture Reform Act of 2000 (P.L. 106-185), improving the federal government's ability to prosecute organized crime cases. Money laundering, the primary method of concealing the illicit proceeds from organized crime activities or placing them back into further illegal activity, was established as a federal criminal offense in the Money Laundering Control Act of 1986 (P.L. 99-570).[28] This Act also established criminal and civil penalties for money laundering, as well as procedures for forfeiting the illicit funds. It appears that these laws have all provided effective tools, as the Department of Justice and Federal Bureau of Investigation have indicated that the three most prominent tools relied upon when investigating and prosecuting organized crime are RICO, money laundering, and asset forfeiture statutes.

More Recent Federal Attention to Organized Crime[29]

Following the terrorist attacks of September 11, 2001, congressional and national law enforcement priorities shifted away from traditional crime fighting toward counterterrorism. More recently, however, there appears to be an increase in national attention to the need for fighting more traditional crime, including organized crime.[30] In fact, after a 15-year hiatus, the Organized Crime Council met in April 2008 for the first time since 1993.[31] The renewed attention to traditional crime fighting—and specifically for purposes of this discussion, organized crime—has increasingly shifted toward the transnational nature of organized crime. Though organized crime has arguably always been transnational, it was not until the 1990s, following the Cold War and the spread of globalization, that the transnational nature of organized crime surged and criminals expanded their operations across increasingly open borders.

Federal Law Enforcement Efforts to Combat Organized Crime

In general, domestic crime control tends to fall on the shoulders of state and local law enforcement agencies. As mentioned above, however, the federal government began to play a larger role in combating organized crime following the enactment of the Omnibus Crime Control and Safe Streets Act of 1968, and even more after RICO and the Organized Crime Control Act of 1970. Various federal agencies are currently involved in controlling the activities of organized crime groups. In addition to domestic efforts to combat organized crime, the federal government is also involved in international efforts.

Domestic Efforts

Combating organized crime is not a task handled by one federal agency or even one department. Many agencies have a hand in tackling the threats posed by organized crime. The Department of Justice, specifically the U.S. Attorney General's Organized Crime Council, is responsible for creating domestic organized crime policy.[32] The Council is chaired by the Deputy Attorney General and has representatives from the Federal Bureau of Investigation (FBI); the U.S. Drug Enforcement Agency (DEA); the Bureau of Alcohol, Tobacco, Firearms and Explosives (ATF); the U.S. Immigration and Customs Enforcement (ICE); the U.S. Secret Service; the Internal Revenue Service (IRS); the U.S. Postal Inspection Service; Diplomatic Security; and the U.S. Department of Labor, Office of the Inspector General.

Although many federal and state departments and agencies are involved in fighting organized crime, the primary agency responsible for combating organized crime is the FBI.[33] The Transnational Criminal Enterprise Section in the Criminal Enterprise Branch of the Criminal Investigative Division is responsible for investigating organized crime. This Organized Crime Section is divided into three principal units investigating (1) La Cosa Nostra, Italian organized crime, and racketeering; (2) Eurasian/Middle Eastern organized crime; and (3) Asian and African criminal enterprises.[34]

As its key analytical tool, the FBI uses the Enterprise Theory of Investigation (ETI) to investigate organized crime. ETI involves two steps: (1) identifying a criminal organization and the criminal activities of this organization and (2) identifying the financial assets of the criminal organization for possible forfeiture.[35] This investigative technique seems to complement the RICO statutes in that both ETI and RICO are aimed at dismantling criminal organizations. Further, ETI identifies financial assets that may be subject to forfeiture under civil RICO statutes. This aspect of ETI is directed at combating money laundering and thus the financial lifeline of organized crime.

Domestic Working Groups and Task Forces[36]

Many of the FBI field offices have organized crime task forces. In those regions, the FBI works with state and local partners as well as with other federal agencies to combat organized crime. These task forces may be broader task forces covering a range of criminal syndicates, or they may be more specific covering a particular organized crime group. One example of a broad organized crime task force exists at the Minneapolis field division of the FBI; this division leads an Organized Crime Task Force that combines the efforts of other federal agencies as well as local law enforcement to target a number of criminal organizations involved in various crimes.[37] On the other hand, examples of more specific organized crime task forces exist at the FBI's New York division; in New York, there have been designated La Cosa Nostra (LCN) task forces, some dedicated to specific LCN families.[38] Even if standing task forces are not formed, domestic agencies work jointly and rely on the resources of one another to combat organized crime. For example, when investigating labor racketeering, the FBI may work with the Department of Labor, the Department of Transportation, and the Internal Revenue Service, as well as state and local authorities.

With respect to prosecuting organized crime cases, the Department of Justice Organized Crime and Racketeering Section has Strike Force Units dedicated to organized crime. These units currently exist in U.S. Attorneys' Offices in 21 of the 93 federal districts with a large organized crime presence. The Strike Force Units operate in these particular 21 offices for historical reasons; those are the 21 offices where the LCN has had the largest presence, and the Strike Force Units continue to operate out of those offices. These units comprise a group of prosecutors with particular expertise in large, multi-defendant RICO cases.[39] Ultimately, the U.S. Attorney General is the chief law enforcement officer responsible for criminal investigations and prosecutions, including those of organized crime.

International Efforts

The United Nations Convention Against Transnational Organized Crime[40] is the main international tool for combating organized crime. In 2005, the United States ratified the Convention as well as the companion Protocols on trafficking in persons and smuggling of migrants. Among other provisions, the Convention provides for greater law enforcement cooperation and mutual legal assistance across nations where there were no previous agreements for such assistance. With the evolving transnational nature of organized crime, this coordination with international organizations is essential. Further, with increasingly open borders and the expansion of the Internet, organized criminals threaten American society not only from within the borders, but beyond.

One outcome of increasing transnational crime is that domestic federal law enforcement agencies work with international organizations to combat organized crime threats to the United States. As one example of this cooperation, the U.S. government and federal agencies support the United Nations (UN) Office of Drugs and Crime (UNODC) efforts to combat international organized crime. UNODC helps UN member countries implement provisions of the Convention Against Transnational Organized Crime to counter organized crime problems. Within the Department of Justice, the U.S. National Central Bureau (USNCB) of the International Criminal Police Organization (INTERPOL)[41] is the point of contact for INTERPOL matters in the United States. The USNCB can access INTERPOL's databases, and it coordinates requests for international investigations between U.S. law enforcement and their international partners.[42] Specifically, the USNCB Terrorism and Violent Crimes Division coordinates requests on organized crime cases. Also, the FBI participates in several international working groups and task forces to formulate best practices in combating organized crime.

International Working Groups and Task Forces

Federal law enforcement agencies in the United States and in Italy participate in the Italian American Working Group, which first met in 1984. This working group addresses problems common to both countries, including organized crime, drug trafficking, money laundering, cyber crime, and extradition issues. The Pantheon Project furthers the law enforcement relationship between the United States and Italy. The Project provides for two FBI agents that work at the Italian National Police headquarters and for two Italian officers that work at the FBI.

With respect to Russian organized crime, the FBI is involved in international *working groups*, including the Eurasian Organized Crime Working Group, the Central European Working Group, and the Southern European Cooperative Initiative. In addition, the FBI set up a joint FBI/Hungarian National Police task force in Budapest, Hungary, to combat Russian organized crime.[43] This task force was established in 2000 to counter the increasing threat of Russian organized crime and is the only international *task force* in which the FBI is currently involved. The FBI has requested additional funding for this task force in its 2011-2015 budget. The FBI, in conjunction with other law enforcement agencies around the world, has also provided INTERPOL with information on individuals involved in Eurasian organized crime; this information is the basis for *Project Millennium*, a multinational effort, led by INTERPOL, to combat Eurasian organized crime.

Federal Investigations and Prosecutions of Organized Crime

According to the Department of Justice and the FBI, the threats posed by organized crime have become more broad and complex than ever before. Federal resources dedicated to organized crime matters, however, do not appear to have expanded along with the threats, and have actually decreased since 2001. After the September 11, 2001, terrorist attacks, national priorities, including those of federal law enforcement, shifted further toward counterterrorism-related activities and further away from traditional crime fighting activities. Within the law enforcement domain, this shift can be objectively seen in the field agents assigned to organized crime casework, the cases investigated, and the cases handled by the U.S. Attorneys' Offices.

Agent Utilization

Following the September 11, 2001, terrorist attacks, the FBI reorganized, prioritizing counterterrorism and counterintelligence over traditional crime matters. The FBI did not, however, significantly change its field agent allocation for organized crime matters between FY2001 and FY2004. Agent allocation remained nearly constant at 700, 697, 698, and 720 agents, respectively, for FY2001-FY2004.[44] On the other hand, the FBI *utilization* of field agents in organized crime matters during this time period did not mirror that of the agent *allocation*. **Figure 1** illustrates that the allocation of agents remained relatively constant, while the actual utilization decreased. The Department of Justice, Office of the Inspector General (OIG), found that in FY2004 the FBI utilized 35% fewer agents on organized crime matters than it did in FY2000.[45] While the FBI utilized 682 agents on organized crime matters in FY2000, this number dropped to 446 in FY2004. The questions remain, however, whether field agents continue to be *allocated* to organized crime matters at similar rates to those before the terrorist attacks of September 11, 2001, and subsequent FBI reorganization, and whether these agents continue to be *utilized* at lower rates than which they are allocated.[46]

This disparity between FBI field agent allocation and field agent utilization may suggest several things. For one, it may suggest that organized crime posed less of a threat to the United States in 2004 than it did in 2000. However, recent actions and testimony by former Attorney General Michael Mukasey suggest the opposite may be true. Former Attorney General Mukasey reconvened the Organized Crime Council in April 2008, for the first time in 15 years.[47] He stated that he did so because organized crime—both domestic and international—remains a significant threat. The sustained threat does not explain the decrease in field agent utilization in these matters. A second possible reason for the disparity in field agent allocation and utilization is that although the FBI did not intend to decrease its agent utilization on organized crime matters, agents may have been diverted to higher-priority issues such as counterterrorism. In fact, the Department of Justice, OIG, reported that the FBI confirmed underutilizing organized crime resources because the field divisions committed to prioritizing counterterrorism first and foremost. The FBI diverted agents from traditional crime squads—such as organized crime—and moved them to counterterrorism squads.[48] A third potential explanation is that the FBI lacks the man-power and monetary resources to address all significant threats that the country faces. This lack of resources may act in conjunction with the FBI's prioritization of counterterrorism. FBI Director Robert Muller has stated that indeed resources have shifted away from traditional crime fighting, and that there is a need to restore the criminal programs to "appropriate resource levels."[49]

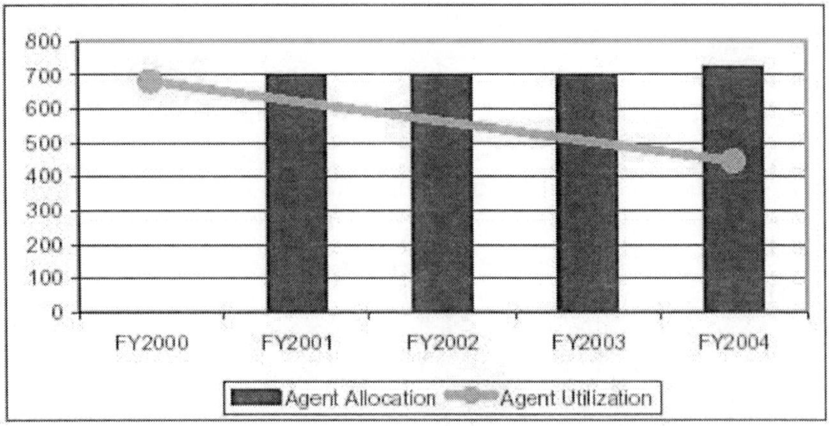

Source: U.S. Department of Justice, Office of the Inspector General, Audit Division, *The External Effects of the Federal Bureau of Investigation's Reprioritization Efforts*, Audit Report 05-37, September 2005, pp. 73-75, http://www.usdoj.gov/oig/reports/FBI/a0537/final.pdf.

Notes: The data on organized crime agent allocation come from the OIG analysis of FBI Resource Management and Allocation (RMA) Office data. The data on organized crime agent utilization come from the OIG analysis of FBI Time Utilization Recordkeeping (TURK) data. The FBI utilized 35% fewer agents on organized crime matters in FY2004 than it did in FY2000. FBI organized crime agent allocation data were not available to the OIG for FY2000 because prior to FY2001, the FBI allocated organized crime and drug resources together.

Figure 1. FBI Allocation and Utilization of Agents on Organized Crime Matters, FY2000-FY2004

Case Openings

In FY2000, the FBI had 682 field agents investigating organized crime, and they initiated (opened) 433 organized crime investigations (cases) in that year, as shown in **Table 1**. Thus, the number of cases per agent was about 0.6. In FY2004, the FBI had 433 field agents investigating organized crime, and they initiated 263 organized crime investigations. Therefore, the number of cases per agent was also about 0.6.[50] Taken alone, a decrease in the number of organized crime cases could suggest that the threat from organized crime is actually decreasing. However, the number of agents investigating organized crime decreased proportionally to the number of organized crime cases opened. Therefore, using data from the number of organized crime case openings does not alone provide a reliable indication of the organized crime threat. There are several possible explanations for the simultaneous decrease in agents investigating organized crime matters and the number of organized crime case openings. One possibility is that a reduction in organized crime activity—and thus a reduction in the number of organized crime cases opened—could lead to fewer agents needed to investigate organized crime matters. On the other hand, a reduction in agents working on organized crime cases could lead to a reduction in the overall number of these cases opened and may not actually reflect a decrease in organized crime activity. One possible side effect of a decrease in the number of federal agents investigating organized crime may be an increased workload for each agent working on these cases; if the organized crime threat is sustained—as has been suggested by DOJ officials—it is possible that the caseloads of organized crime agents could increase if the number of agents actually investigating organized crime is sustained or further decreased.[51]

Table 1. FBI Organized Crime Cases Worked Per Agent, FY2000 and FY2004

Fiscal Year	Organized Crime Agent Utilization	Number of Organized Crime Cases Opened	Organized Crime Cases/Agent
2000	682	433	0.63
2004	446	263	0.59

Source: U.S. Department of Justice, Office of the Inspector General, Audit Division, *The External Effects of the Federal Bureau of Investigation's Reprioritization Efforts*, Audit Report 05-37, September 2005, pp. 73-75, http://www.usdoj.gov/oig/reports/FBI/a0537/final.pdf.

Notes: Data on organized crime agent utilization and case openings include data across the FBI's three organized crime subprograms: (1) La Cosa Nostra and Italian, (2) Asian, and (3) Russian and Eurasian. The data on organized crime agent utilization come from the OIG analysis of FBI Time Utilization Recordkeeping (TURK) data. The data on organized crime case openings come from the OIG analysis of FBI Automated Case Support (ACS) data. There was about a 35% decrease in the number of FBI agents utilized on organized crime matters and about a 39% decrease in the number of organized crime cases opened between FY2000 and FY2004.

Prosecutions

The Department of Justice, Organized Crime and Racketeering Section (OCRS), oversees federal organized crime prosecutions. As noted earlier, OCRS has organized crime Strike Force Units in 21 of the 94 U.S. Attorneys' Offices (USAOs) where there exists a large organized crime presence in that district. **Figure 2** graphs the number of organized crime cases referred to the USAOs for prosecution from FY1999 through FY2008. As evidenced in the figure, there has not been a consistent increase or decrease in the number of organized crime cases filed with the USAOs across these years.

Many factors could influence the number of organized crime cases referred to the USAOs for prosecution. While this number could reflect the actual activities of organized crime groups, several factors suggest that the trends in prosecutions may not mirror the trends in organized criminal activity—either in type or in number. Firstly, prosecutions may be driven in part by Administration priorities, which may not emphasize all federal crimes equally. Secondly, organized crime cases that are actually prosecuted are only a small subset (and not necessarily a proportionate subset) of those crimes committed.[52] Therefore, the number of organized crime prosecutions alone provides little evidence as to the true trends in organized criminal activity.

One question that remains is whether the resources and tools for investigating and prosecuting organized crime in the United States—as previously provided by Congress—are the most effective tools for combating today's threats from organized crime.

CURRENT ORGANIZED CRIME TRENDS

As mentioned, organized crime in the United States has taken on an increasingly transnational nature. This shift has been facilitated by factors such as economic globalization and improved communications technology.[53] The section below provides a detailed discussion of the organized crime groups that operate in the United States, the activities of these groups, and the domestic industries that have been and may continue to be threatened by organized crime.

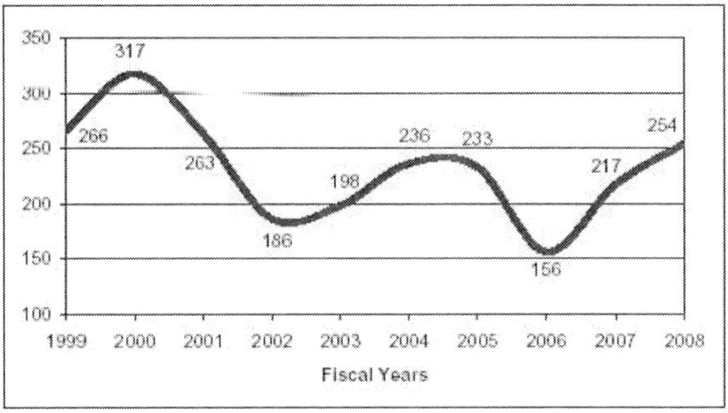

Source: Data provided to CRS by the USAO.

Notes: These data include organized crime cases filed with the USAOs from all federal agencies.

Figure 2. Organized Crime Cases Filed with the U.S. Attorneys' Offices, FY1999-FY2008

Source: The FBI identifies and provides an overview of these various organized crime groups on its website at http://www.fbi.gov/hq/cid/orgcrime/ocshome.htm.

Figure 3. Organized Crime Threats in the United States

One way of analyzing the organized crime threat is by examining the most prominent organized crime groups operating in the United States. The FBI, for instance, provides information on the various organized crime groups in order to present a picture of organized crime in the United States. A second method is by examining those areas of society threatened most by the activities of organized crime (such as the economy or national security), regardless of which group is committing the crime. The Organized Crime and Racketeering Section (OCRS) at DOJ, for example, presents the organized crime threats to the United States in terms of the principal threat areas, rather than the individual groups committing crimes. Subsequent discussion uses both approaches to analyze organized crime.

Organized Crime Groups Operating in the United States[54]

Although organized crime is popularly associated with the Italian Mafia, the breadth of organized crime in the United States includes many other criminal organizations. The FBI investigates organized crime groups that fall into three major categories: (1) La Cosa Nostra, Italian organized crime, and racketeering; (2) Eurasian/Middle Eastern organized crime; and (3) Asian and African criminal enterprises.[55] **Figure 3** outlines the top organized crime threats to the United States, as identified by the FBI. Threats to the United States posed by selected large-scale criminal organizations are discussed below.

Eurasian/Russian

The discussion of Russian organized crime tends to reference not only Russian crime syndicates, but a variety of Eurasian crime groups as well.[56] These groups began emerging in the United States in the late 1970s and became even more prevalent following the collapse of the Soviet Union in 1991. They are now considered by the FBI to be the top organized crime threat to the United States.[57] The Russian organized crime groups that operate in the United States exhibit less of a traditional hierarchical structure than the Italian Cosa Nostra, and they form their networks based more on the skills needed for particular crimes.[58] In the United States, Russian organized criminals are involved in long-established organized crime activities such as extortion, abduction, human smuggling, prostitution, drug trafficking, and theft, as well as white-collar criminal activities including money laundering and fraud of various types. In fact, the FBI has indicated that roughly 60% of FBI cases targeting Russian organized crime involve fraud.[59] The types of fraud and scams that Russian criminals participate in cross industries from health care and strategic commodities (e.g., precious metals) fraud to credit card, insurance, securities, and investment fraud. They are also involved in scams in domains such as tax evasion and energy price rigging. Many Russian organized crime groups operate in New York, New Jersey, Boston, Philadelphia, Chicago, Los Angeles, San Francisco, and Miami, among other cities.[60]

U.S. law enforcement has relied heavily on RICO, money laundering, and asset forfeiture statutes to prosecute Russian crime syndicates. They consider these pieces of legislation as significant for combating organized crime activities as well as the structure of the criminal organizations.[61] Principal efforts to control Russian organized crime groups include the establishment of both domestic and international task forces and working groups aimed at dismantling these crime syndicates. Domestically, the FBI has set up *task forces* in cities such as New York, New Jersey, Philadelphia, Chicago, San Francisco, Los Angeles, and Miami. Also, local police departments in major cities, including New York and Los Angeles, have set up Russian organized crime task forces.[62] In addition, the FBI is involved in international *working groups* concerned with Russian organized crime, including the Eurasian Organized Crime Working Group; the Central European Working Group at the International Law Enforcement Academy in Budapest, Hungary; and the Southern European Cooperative Initiative in Bucharest, Romania. The FBI is also involved in an international organized crime *task force* in Budapest, Hungary, aimed at combating Russian organized crime; currently, this is the only international task force aimed at combating organized crime in which the FBI is involved. The FBI has indicated that this international effort has been invaluable in developing international partnerships and intelligence, as well as expanding its international capabilities.[63]

Asian

Asian organized crime groups have had a presence in the United States since at least the early 1900s. However, there has been an increase in Asian organized crime since the 1990s.[64] Research indicates that there is not one unified Asian organized crime group; rather, there exist numerous crime syndicates, some more traditionally organized than others.[65] According to the FBI, traditional groups include Chinese triads from Hong Kong, Taiwan, and Macau, and the Japanese Yakuza. Less traditional groups include tongs, triads, and Asian street gangs such as the Big Circle and the Fuk Ching. Similar to a trend seen among Russian organized crime groups, an emerging trend seen among Asian crime syndicates is a willingness to cooperate across ethnic and racial lines if it is profitable for the enterprise. Asian organized crime groups derive most of their profits from trafficking in drugs—such as heroin—and people, but are also actively involved in other criminal activities, from money laundering, counterfeiting, and fraud to kidnapping and the theft of autos, software, and clothing. The FBI indicates that Boston, Chicago, Honolulu, Las Vegas, Los Angeles, New Orleans, New York, Newark, Philadelphia, Portland, San Francisco, Seattle, and Washington, D.C,. are examples of areas with a high prevalence of Asian organized crime.

U.S. law enforcement has relied heavily on RICO, money laundering, and asset forfeiture statutes to prosecute Asian crime syndicates. Similar to efforts aimed at combating Russian organized crime groups, U.S. law enforcement participates in domestic and international working groups aimed at combating Asian organized crime. Domestically, the Interagency Working Group on Alien Smuggling examines policy and investigative issues surrounding the smuggling of aliens and trafficking of women and children, including involvement of Asian organized crime groups in these activities. The FBI is also involved in international working groups concerned with Asian organized crime, including the FBI/National Police Agency of Japan Working Group, Interpol's Project Bridge, the International Asian Organized Crime Conference, the Canadian/United States Cross-Border Crime Forum, and the International Law Enforcement Academy in Bangkok, Thailand.[66]

Italian

The La Cosa Nostra (LCN), is the most prominent Italian organized crime group operating in the United States.[67] Within the LCN, there are five principal crime *families.*[68] The LCN is involved in an array of illegal activities, from gambling and loan sharking to drug trafficking and money laundering, that threaten American society.[69] Most members of the LCN operate in the New York metropolitan area, but there are also criminal operations in Boston, Chicago, Newark, Detroit, Philadelphia, and Miami.[70] La Cosa Nostra has been operating in the United States since the 1920s and still poses a threat today.

Early congressional and law enforcement efforts to control organized crime were aimed directly at controlling the illegal activities of the Mafia (LCN). As discussed earlier, these early congressional efforts involved enacting the 1968 Omnibus Crime Control and Safe Streets Act (P.L. 90-351) and the 1970 Organized Crime Control Act and RICO (P.L. 91-452), as well as the asset forfeiture and money laundering statutes. Civil RICO lawsuits have been particularly effective in purging the LCN from legitimate industries and unions, such as the Las Vegas gaming industry, the New York moving and storage industries, and the union representing truckers servicing JFK airport in New York.[71] In addition to federal RICO statutes, many states have also adopted RICO statues. Many believe that RICO has been the most powerful tool in combating La Cosa Nostra.[72] Despite these effective tools, the LCN remains a major organized crime threat to American society.

Balkan

The FBI identifies Balkan organized crime, and Albanian groups in particular, as among the most formidable organized crime groups today, as evidenced, in part, by an increase in Albanian-born individuals arrested in the United States.[73] Albanian organized crime groups emerged in the United States in the late 1980s and have evolved from being close knit families to allowing in outsiders with particular areas of criminal expertise. These groups are active in areas such as New York, Los Angeles, Las Vegas, Dallas, and Houston, to name a few. Balkan crime groups have been involved in various illegal activities such as gambling, extortion, robbery, counterfeit currency, drug trafficking, human smuggling, real estate fraud, money laundering, witness intimidation, and murder.

One emerging trend seen among Balkan organized crime groups is an increased cooperation with other organized crime groups—further evidence that Balkan organized crime is not just increasing, but expanding.[74] For example, the FBI has indicated that the LCN has partnered with Albanian organized crime in New York. There, the LCN is relying on the Albanians as their enforcers, and the Albanians have increasingly taken over some turf there that was previously dominated by the LCN.

Other Organized Crime Groups

The federal government recognizes threats from other organized crime groups that may not have the same notoriety as larger groups such as the LCN. For example, Middle Eastern Criminal Enterprises are primarily involved in organized theft, financial fraud, money laundering, and cigarette smuggling. Also, African crime syndicates—and particularly Nigerian groups—are involved in heroin trafficking, money laundering, and fraud (including insurance, bank, auto, healthcare, identity, and document fraud).

Of note, a trend among organized crime groups is that they begin by victimizing members of their own neighborhoods and ethnic communities, and then expand their illegal activities beyond these community lines. For example, in the 1920s Prohibition era, the Italian-American mafia began victimizing other Italians in the Five Points neighborhood of Little Italy in New York, before extending their activities to other neighborhoods of New York and the surrounding metropolitan area.[75] If this is indeed a common pattern across organized crime groups, then it is likely that emerging crime groups may expand their activities rather than restrict them to the areas in which they currently operate.

Domestic Impact of Organized Crime

The U.S. Department of Justice Organized Crime Council,[76] chaired by the Deputy U.S. Attorney General, has identified eight strategic threats to the United States posed by international organized crime.[77] Of note, the term "international organized crime" includes not only those organized crime groups operating outside the borders of the United States, but within the U.S. borders as well. As mentioned earlier, the Council noted that international organized criminals have and may penetrate the energy and other strategic sectors of the economy; provide logistical and other support to terrorists, foreign intelligence services, and governments; smuggle/traffic people and contraband goods into the United States; exploit the United States and international financial system to move illicit funds; use cyberspace to target U.S. victims and infrastructure; manipulate securities exchanges and perpetrate sophisticated frauds; corrupt or seek to corrupt public officials in the United States and abroad; and use violence or the threat of violence as a basis for power.

Former U.S. Attorney General Michael Mukasey outlined strategic goals in combating these threats. These goals continue to include

- targeting the largest organized crime threats,
- dismantling criminal organizations and removing their leadership,
- marshalling information from all available resources, and
- relying on all possible domestic and international tools and law enforcement partnerships.[78]

One specific goal of the Organized Crime Council that may be of particular interest to Congress is to "provide law enforcement with updated legislation and operational procedures needed to combat international organized crime."[79] Specifically, the Organized Crime Council indicated that laws and regulations should be expanded, updated, or modified to afford the government the abilities to investigate and prosecute organized criminals that affect American society from outside U.S. borders. This suggests that federal law enforcement currently may not have the extraterritorial jurisdiction or the most effective tools to combat the evolving organized crime threats to the United States. The section below provides a detailed discussion of some potential impacts of organized crime, followed by possible issues that the 111th Congress may consider.

Impact of Organized Crime on the Economy

Considering the current economic downturn, some analysts may question the effect that organized crime may have on American society. Organized crime could further weaken the economy with illegal activities (such as cigarette trafficking and tax evasion scams) that result in a loss of tax revenue for state and federal governments. Their fraudulent activities in the domains of strategic commodities, credit, insurance, stocks, securities, and investments could further weaken the already-troubled financial and housing markets.

Money Laundering

Money laundering involves concealing the nature, location, source, ownership, or control of proceeds from an illegal activity or placing them back into further illegal activity.[80] The ill-gotten proceeds are laundered through a variety of methods to become "clean money." With the expansion of the Internet and increased globalization, the methods of money laundering continue to become increasingly complex and difficult to detect. The Financial Crimes Enforcement Network (FinCEN), under the Department of the Treasury, indicates that the routes for money laundering include banks, check cashers, money transmitters, businesses, and casinos. Money launderers use methods such as complex wire transfers, shell companies, and currency smuggling to hide their dirty money.[81]

Money laundering became a federal crime in the Money Laundering Control Act of 1986 (P.L. 99-570). It came to Congress's attention that organized criminals were camouflaging their proceeds, and Congress strengthened the federal criminal statues to better combat criminal organizations.[82] Recently, the scope of the money laundering statute has come under examination. The statute prohibits financial transactions of proceeds from illicit activities, but it does not currently define what constitutes "proceeds." The Supreme Court ruled in *United States v. Santos* that in the money laundering statute, the term "proceeds" refers to profits rather than gross receipts.[83]

Legislation has since been introduced in the 111th Congress to amend the money laundering statute. The Money Laundering Correction Act of 2009 (H.R. 1793) and the Money Laundering Control Enhancement Act of 2009 (S. 378) would clarify the statute so that the term "proceeds" includes gross receipts of an illegal activity. The Fraud Enforcement and Recovery Act of 2009 (S. 386) would clarify both the money laundering and international money laundering statutes. Namely, it would indicate that "proceeds" includes gross receipts of illegal activities. Also, it would extend the international money laundering statute to apply to tax evasion in addition to the crimes already included. Some experts have argued that expanding the predicate offenses for international money laundering could broaden the tools the federal government is able to rely upon when investigating and prosecuting organized crime that is increasingly crossing international lines.

Cigarette Trafficking

Law enforcement agencies have also noted that criminal syndicates' participation in the trafficking of contraband cigarettes poses a significant threat to American society. A number of different organized crime groups are involved in cigarette trafficking. This illicit activity indirectly threatens the American economy and American communities. Cigarette smuggling leads to lost tax revenue. Businesses, in turn, compensate by raising taxes for the consumer, ultimately placing the increased economic burden on the consumer.[84] Excessive economic burdens on the consumer are of particular concern now because of the current economic recession. Consequently, revenues that would assist in funding government programs are being illegally redistributed because of organized crime activities.

Piracy and Counterfeiting

There is evidence that organized criminals are becoming increasingly involved in the production and distribution of counterfeit and pirated goods.[85] In Los Angeles County alone, Russian, Asian, Eurasian, and Lebanese organized crime groups are among those that have been involved in intellectual property rights crimes.[86] Industries targeted are broad, including the music and motion picture industries, clothing companies, luxury goods manufacturers, and the tobacco industry. The federal government has taken several steps so far in fighting these crimes. In fact, in March 2004, the Department of Justice created an Intellectual Property Task Force to combat the increase in intellectual property piracy and counterfeiting by organized crime groups. Also, the Office of the United States Trade Representative (USTR) has indicated that an Anti-Counterfeiting Trade Agreement (ACTA) is being formulated with other countries, including Australia, Canada, EU, Japan, Jordan, Korea, Mexico, Morocco, New Zealand, Singapore, Switzerland, and the United Arab Emirates. According to the USTR, one benefit of the ACTA is that it will help combat the piracy and counterfeiting that is an "easy source of revenue for organized crime."[87]

Counterfeit currency is another example of a domain in which many organized crime groups are involved. Asian organized crime groups in Los Angeles and New Jersey have been linked to the production of "supernotes," or fake $50 and $100 bills. This can not only lead to a loss in actual money (for those paid in the counterfeit currency), but it can damage the value of the U.S. dollar.[88] Some experts and policy analysts have suggested that one possible legislative option to help counter the involvement of organized crime in piracy and counterfeiting may be to expand the organized crime and money laundering statutes to include large-scale piracy and counterfeiting tied to other criminal activities.[89]

Organized Crime and Terrorists

In addition to concern surrounding the many industries in which organized criminals operate, both analysts and policymakers have expressed concern about the potential nexus between organized crime and terrorism. The principal distinction authorities make between organized crime groups and terrorist groups is motivation. Money motivates organized crime, and ideology motivates terrorism. Because of this fundamental difference, the National Intelligence Council expects that between now and 2020:

> [T]he relationship between terrorists and organized criminals will remain primarily a matter of business, i.e., that terrorists will turn to criminals who can provide forged documents, smuggled weapons, or clandestine travel assistance when the terrorists cannot procure these goods and services on their own. Organized criminal groups, however, are unlikely to form long-term strategic alliances with terrorists. Organized crime is motivated by the desire to make money and tends to regard any activity beyond that required to effect profit as bad for business. For their part, terrorist leaders are concerned

> that ties to non-ideological partners will increase the chance of successful police penetration or that profits will seduce the faithful.[90]

Despite the difference in motivation for organized crime and terrorism, the linking element for the two is money. Terrorist organizations may obtain funding from criminal acts, similar to organized crime groups. Also, terrorist organizations may launder these funds, similar to criminal organizations.[91] One example of a domain in which both organized criminals and terrorists may both benefit monetarily is piracy. Although there is currently less evidence of terrorist involvement in piracy, this business is a high-profit, low-risk activity, attractive to both criminals and terrorists.[92]

Even if organized crime groups and terrorist organizations do not form long-term alliances, the possibility of short-term business alliances may be of concern to citizens and policymakers alike. The FBI indicates that although it has not yet had a case of organized crime groups working directly with terrorists, the possibility exists, and it continue to be watchful for this nexus. Because organized criminals are monetarily motivated, the FBI believes that these criminals would be inclined to work with terrorists if offered sufficient funds.[93]

Although there are few reported instances of organized crime groups *actually* aiding terrorists, there are reported instances of international organized criminals *conspiring* to provide support to terrorist organizations. One such instance is Viktor Bout, an international arms trafficker who has been charged with conspiring to sell weapons to the Revolutionary Armed Forces of Columbia (FARC).[94] As mentioned earlier in this report, federal law enforcement distinguishes between organized crime groups and drug trafficking organizations. Although there are no reported instances of organized crime groups directly working with terrorists, there are reported instances of "narco-terrorism," or terrorism funded through the proceeds of drug trafficking; the Liberation Tigers of Tamil Eelam, members of Hizbollah, and the Al-Qaida network are all examples of terrorist groups with close ties to drug trafficking.[95] GAO reports that U.S. officials are concerned with the threat in Eurasia of the links between terrorist organizations and organized crime, and trafficking in persons and drugs.[96] With the prevalence of drug trafficking in the United States (via drug trafficking organizations as well as via organized crime groups that also have a hand in drug trafficking), policymakers may question (1) to what extent there is a nexus between domestic organized crime and terrorism and (2) what measures will most effectively combat both terrorism and organized crime.

Potential Issues for Congress

The evolving nature of organized crime, as discussed, presents several issues that Congress may wish to consider. One issue is whether the tools that Congress has provided the federal government with to investigate and prosecute domestic organized crime—namely RICO, money laundering, and asset forfeiture statutes—are still effective tools to combat today's threats from organized crime. As evidenced by proposed legislation, Congress is considering clarifying and expanding these statutes so as to better equip the federal government to fight organized crime.

Federal Organized Crime Resources

Policies exist that allow federal law enforcement to investigate and prosecute organized crime groups. What may not fully exist, however, are the monetary and personnel resources to effectively combat organized crime—evidenced by a decrease in FBI agents used to investigate organized crime matters and in FBI organized crime case openings.

As previously discussed, in FY2004, the FBI utilized about 35% fewer agents on organized crime matters than it did in FY2000. The FBI has recognized that prioritizing counterterrorism and counterintelligence cases affects resources available to criminal investigations and that targeting the most significant threats will allow criminal investigative resources to be used most effectively. FBI Director Robert Muller testified to the need for restoring resources to the FBI's criminal programs, which include organized crime.[97] Efforts—both administrative and congressional—can be made to this effect in several ways. One congressional option may be to increase overall funding available to the FBI and other federal law enforcement agencies that may be experiencing a decrease in resources dedicated to more traditional crime fighting matters, including organized crime. If these resources are then administratively allocated to criminal programs, organized crime agent utilization could potentially be more closely aligned with agent allocation without taking resources away from higher priority areas. Another congressional option may be to provide directed funding for organized crime matters. This option could ensure that any increase in funding intended to be directed toward criminal programs or organized crime matters would be utilized in those domains.

Yet another policy option may be to decide that the existing resources dedicated to organized crime are sufficient, given the limited financial resources available under the federal budget and given the national priority of combating the threats from terrorism. If, on the other hand, more funding were available or if the link between organized crime and terrorism were more direct, the case for reevaluating the funding directed toward organized crime might be stronger. However, considering the current budget constraints and priorities, some may consider existing organized crime funding as adequate.

Multilateral Crime Fighting

The federal government is already involved in several multilateral efforts—with state and local agencies as well as with international allies—to combat organized crime. With respect to working with domestic state and local law enforcement agencies, federal law enforcement agencies have formed joint task forces, some that target a variety of organized crime groups and some that target specific criminal organizations. Several of these task forces were outlined in previous sections of this report. Some analysts have suggested that despite the benefits of multilateral crime fighting, potential jurisdictional issues may arise. As organized crime groups have expanded their activities beyond state and even national lines, so has the responsibility for combating organized crime expanded. There exists a clear line between state and federal jurisdiction for prosecuting crimes. However, jurisdiction over agency responsibility for investigating cases may at times be unclear. This may be due in part to overlapping agency responsibilities and may also arise from the complexity of the cases investigated. For instance, an organized crime case with a drug component may fall under the jurisdiction of both the FBI and the DEA, potentially causing confusion on which agency would take the lead on such cases.

An issue that may become more visible than the issue of domestic law enforcement coordination is that of international law enforcement coordination. By ratifying the United Nations Convention Against Transnational Organized Crime in 2005, Congress took a step in working with foreign governments and law enforcement agencies to combat organized crime. Specifically, this Convention provided the framework for international cooperation by requiring mutual legal assistance between countries in fighting organized crime, as well as by requiring extradition for those organized criminal offenses outlined in the Convention. These provisions enhance the

United States' ability to combat international organized crime and work with countries where there was no previous mutual assistance arrangement already in place.[98]

As organized crime becomes increasingly transnational, so may the need for international organized crime working groups, task forces, and law enforcement cooperation. The benefits of international cooperation and partnerships are twofold. U.S. law enforcement can extend its expertise and capabilities to assist overseas law enforcement combat organized crime. Partnering with international law enforcement will develop the intelligence needed to support domestic investigations of organized crime.[99] However, one of the challenges, as expressed by federal law enforcement, is the increased time required to conduct international investigations.[100] Among the various effects that this may have on investigations, organized crime groups may be inadvertently afforded a longer time to conduct their illegal activities, potentially affecting a greater number of victims or increasing the magnitude of damage to the victims. A second challenge relating to international investigations may arise from the domestic practice that federal prosecutors are involved at all stages of organized crime cases. When investigations are conducted abroad, the involvement of prosecutors may not be as consistent.

In addition to law enforcement collaboration with foreign nations, Congress has given the federal government extraterritorial jurisdiction to investigate and prosecute individuals who criminally violate U.S. interests abroad (P.L. 99-399).[101] This legislation was directed at combating terrorist acts against the United States, and thus the extraterritorial jurisdiction does not necessarily cover all crimes committed by organized crime groups. The increasingly transnational nature of organized crime as well as the potential for a nexus between organized crime and terrorism—as suggested by some analysts—may lead policymakers to question whether and/or how to extend this extraterritorial jurisdiction beyond the crimes currently covered with the practical and diplomatic challenges that such an approach may entail.

Potential Organized Crime Nexus with Terrorism

Some experts have indicated that the lines between organized crime groups and terrorist organizations may become increasingly blurry.[102] Even if organized crime groups and terrorist organizations do not form "long-term strategic alliances," as suggested by the National Security Council,[103] the links between organized crime and terrorism may still be significant. The Council suggests (as does the FBI), however, that organized criminals and terrorists may ally for business purposes. Both criminal and terrorist organizations depend on money; organized criminals are profit-driven, and terrorists—though ideology-driven—need money and goods to finance their operations. It has been suggested that organized crime groups may cooperate with terrorists if the business alliance is profitable.

Some experts have cited potential additional areas of overlap between organized crime groups and terrorist organizations. For example, the language school that provided some visas for the 9/11 hijackers is also reported to have provided visas for prostitutes of a human trafficking ring.[104] There have also been instances of terrorist organizations drawing on the structure and activities of organized crime groups as models for structuring their organizations and financing their operations. Drug trafficking, for instance, has been one of the most profitable activities for both organized crime groups and terrorist organizations. Other illegal activities include human trafficking, weapons trafficking, endangered species trafficking, art and antique theft, counterfeiting, and credit card fraud.[105]

Because there may be overlap between organized crime groups and terrorist organizations in terms of their criminal activities and funding sources, some analysts have argued that combating organized crime is central to combating terrorism.[106] Congress therefore may consider the potential nexus between organized crime and terrorism when addressing the nation's security and determining the appropriate allocation and utilization of resources, as well as effective information sharing and interagency cooperation, as discussed above.

LEGISLATION IN THE 111TH CONGRESS

The Public Corruption Prosecution Improvements Act (S. 49), as introduced in the Senate, would among other things, expand the RICO statute by expanding the list of predicate offenses for racketeering. In particular, provisions of this Act would include "embezzlement or theft of public money, property, or records" as well as "theft or bribery concerning programs receiving Federal funds" in the list of RICO predicate offenses. Further, this Act would authorize evidence of these two crimes as a legal basis for the FBI or other investigative agency with jurisdiction to institute a wiretap. Although this bill is intended to combat public corruption in general, it would also expand the federal government's ability to investigate and prosecute organized crime and would extend to instances where public officials may be corrupted by organized crime.

Several bills in the 111th Congress are directly aimed at combating money laundering. As mentioned before, in *United States v. Santos*, the U.S. Supreme Court ruled that in the money laundering statute, the term "proceeds" refers to profits rather than gross receipts.[107] Two bills in the 111th Congress would amend this statute. The Money Laundering Correction Act of 2009 (H.R. 1793), as introduced in the House; the Money Laundering Control Enhancement Act of 2009 (S. 378), as introduced in the Senate; and the Fraud Enforcement and Recovery Act of 2009 (S. 386), as favorably reported by the Senate Committee on the Judiciary, would all amend the money laundering statute so that the term "proceeds" includes gross receipts of an illegal activity. S. 386 would also extend the international money laundering statute to apply to tax evasion (via moving money outside of the United States) in addition to the crimes already included.

End Notes

[1] U.S. Department of Justice, "Remarks prepared for delivery by Attorney General Michael B. Mukasey on International Organized Crime at the Center for Strategic and International Studies," press release, April 23, 2008, http://www.usdoj.gov/ag/speeches/2008/ag-speech-080425.html.

[2] Ibid. The Organized Crime Council began meeting in 1970 and continued through 1993. When former Attorney General Michael Mukasey reconvened the Council in 2008, this was the first time it had met in 15 years.

[3] Department of Justice, Office of the Inspector General, Audit Division, *The External Effects of the Federal Bureau of Investigation's Reprioritization Efforts*, Audit Report 05-37, September 2005, p. 73. This statement is based on statistics from the FBI alone, not including other federal law enforcement agencies. The FBI is the federal law enforcement agency most involved in investigating organized crime matters.

[4] James O. Finckenauer, "Problems of Definition: What is Organized Crime?" *Trends in Organized Crime*, vol. 8, no. 3 (Spring 2005), pp. 63-82.

[5] According to the FBI, there are four main Italian organized crime groups operating in the United States: the Sicilian Mafia (from which the LCN was formed), the Camorra or Neapolitan Mafia, the 'Ndrangheta or Calabrian Mafia, and the Sacra Corona Unita or United Sacred Crown. The term "Mafia" tends to be an encapsulating term referencing all of these groups.

[6] Federal law enforcement tends to refer to organized crime groups as distinct from drug trafficking organizations (DTOs) or gangs. Therefore, this report does not include specific discussions of DTOs or gangs. For more information on DTOs (Mexican DTOs, in particular), see the archived CRS Report RL34215, *Mexico's Drug Cartels*, by Colleen W. Cook. For more information on gangs, see CRS Report RL341 12, *Gangs in Central America*, by Clare Ribando Seelke; CRS Report RL34233, *The MS-13 and 18th Street Gangs: Emerging Transnational Gang Threats?* by Celinda Franco; and archived CRS Report RL33400, *Youth Gangs: Background, Legislation, and Issues*, by Celinda Franco.

[7] RICO is codified at 18 U.S.C. § 1961-1968.

[8] As defined in 18 U.S.C. § 1961, an "'enterprise' includes any individual, partnership, corporation, association, or other legal entity, and any union or group of individuals associated ... although not [necessarily] a legal entity," and a "'pattern of racketeering activity' requires at least two acts of racketeering activity" to occur within 10 years of one another for a criminal organization to be prosecuted for racketeering. Racketeering is defined as any number of violations, including an act or threat involving murder, kidnapping, gambling, arson, robbery, bribery, extortion, or dealing in a controlled substance. See 18 U.S.C. § 1961 for a comprehensive list of the predicate offenses for racketeering.

[9] Frank Browning and John Gerassi, *The American Way of Crime* (New York: G.P. Putnam & Sons, 1980), p. 53.

[10] U.S. Congress, House Government Operations, Legal and Monetary Affairs, *Federal Effort Against Organized Crime: Report of Agency Operations*, committee print, 90th Cong., 2nd sess., June 1968.

[11] Congressional testimony in 1963 by Joseph Valachi—a prominent member of the LCN Genovese crime family— shed light on the true extent of the LCN network. Joseph Valachi was the first Mafia member to publicly affirm the existence of a criminal organization such as the LCN. In 1963, he testified before the Permanent Subcommittee on Investigations of the Senate Committee on Government Operations. For text of his complete testimony, please see U.S. Congress, Senate Committee on Government Operations, Permanent Subcommittee on Investigations, *Organized Crime and Illicit Traffic in Narcotics*, 88th Cong., 1st sess., September 25, 1963.

[12] Task Force on Organized Crime, *Task Force Report: Organized Crime: Annotations and Consultants' Papers*, The President's Commission on Law Enforcement and Administration of Justice, Washington, 1967, p. 14.

[13] From remarks by Rep. Dante B. Fascell, Chairman, in U.S. Congress, House Committee on Government Operations, Subcommittee on Legal and Monetary Affairs, *The Federal Effort Against Organized Crime. Part 1*, 90th Cong., 1st sess., April 5, 1967.

[14] From remarks by Fred M. Vinson, Jr., Assistant Attorney General, Criminal Division, Department of Justice, in U.S. Congress, House Committee on Government Operations, Subcommittee on Legal and Monetary Affairs, *The Federal Effort Against Organized Crime. Part 1*, 90th Cong., 1st sess., April 5, 1967.

[15] For this analysis, CRS used the data referenced in the U.S. Congress, House Committee on Government Operations, Subcommittee on Legal and Monetary Affairs, *The Federal Effort Against Organized Crime. Part 1*, 90th Cong., 1st sess., April 5, 1967. Convictions carry a greater burden of proof than indictments, and thus are more difficult for prosecutors to obtain. While the raw numbers of both indictments and convictions were on the rise, the *proportion* of indicted individuals who were later convicted decreased; this may suggest that organized crime was perhaps growing at a rate faster than the criminal justice system was able to handle.

[16] Task Force on Organized Crime, *Organized Crime: Report of the Task Force on Organized Crime*, National Advisory Committee on Criminal Justice Standards and Goals, Washington, 1976.

[17] U.S. Congress, Senate Committee on the Judiciary, *Organized Crime Control Act of 1969*, report to accompany S. 30, 91st Cong., 1st sess., December 16, 1969, S.Rept. 91-617.

[18] The LEAA administered federal funding for state and local law enforcement agencies, educational programs, research, and crime initiatives. It is no longer in existence and has since been succeeded by the Office of Justice Programs (OJP).

[19] The Omnibus Crime Control and Safe Streets Act was later amended by the Violent Crime Control and Law Enforcement Act of 1994. This amended Act addressed organized crime in that it expressed the sense of the Senate that "the United States should encourage the development of a United Nations Convention on Organized Crime." Five years later in 1999, the United Nations began developing a Convention against Transnational Organized

Crime. The Omnibus Crime Control and Safe Streets Act was also amended by the Electronic Communications Privacy Act (ECPA) of 1986 (P.L. 99-508), which substantially revised Title III and related provisions. For more information on the ECPA, see CRS Report 98-326, *Privacy: An Overview of Federal Statutes Governing Wiretapping and Electronic Eavesdropping*, by Gina Stevens and Charles Doyle.

[20] Remarks from Sen. John L. McClellan, U.S. Congress, House Judiciary, No. 5, *Organized Crime Control*, 91st Cong., 2nd sess., May 20, 1970.

[21] Remarks from John N. Mitchell, Attorney General of the United States, U.S. Congress, House Judiciary, No. 5, *Organized Crime Control*, 91st Cong., 2nd sess., May 21, 1970.

[22] 18 U.S.C. § 3521. Although the foundation for the Witness Security Program was authorized by the Organized Crime Control Act of 1970, the program was established under Part F of Chapter XII of P.L. 98-473.

[23] RICO is codified at 18 U.S.C. § 1961-1968. For more information on RICO, please see CRS Report 96-950, *RICO: A Brief Sketch*, by Charles Doyle.

[24] See Howard Abadinsky, *Organized Crime*, 7th ed. (Belmont, CA: Wadsworth, 2003).

[25] See 18 U.S.C. § 1961 for a comprehensive list of the predicate offenses for racketeering. Offenses include—but are not limited to—crimes such as murder, kidnapping, gambling, arson, robbery, bribery, extortion, dealing in obscene matter, dealing in a controlled substance or listed chemical, counterfeiting, theft from interstate shipment, embezzlement from pension and welfare funds, embezzlement from union funds, fraud and related activity in connection with identification documents or access devices, mail fraud, wire fraud, financial institution fraud, procurement of citizenship or nationalization unlawfully, obstruction of justice or criminal investigations, tampering with or retaliating against a witness, false statements or forgery in application and use of a passport or other documents, peonage, slavery, trafficking in persons, interference with commerce, and laundering of monetary instruments.

[26] Federal Bureau of Investigation, "Move Over, Mafia: The New Face of Organized Crime," press release, February 13, 2009, http://www.fbi.gov/page2/feb09/organizedcrime_021309.html.

[27] For more information on forfeiture, see CRS Report 97-139, *Crime and Forfeiture*, by Charles Doyle. Forfeiture comes in two forms: civil and criminal. Both result in the confiscation of property derived from or used in criminal activities. Criminal forfeiture is confiscation accomplished as part of the prosecution of the property owner. Civil forfeiture is accomplished through a civil proceeding ordinarily brought against the property involved in the illicit activity.

[28] Money laundering is codified at 18 U.S.C. § 1956. The Money Laundering Control Act is Subtitle H of Title I of the Anti-Drug Abuse Act of 1986. For more information on the federal money laundering statutes, see CRS Report RL33315, *Money Laundering: An Overview of 18 U.S.C. 1956 and Related Federal Criminal Law*, by Charles Doyle and Todd Garvey.

[29] In addition to the legislative efforts to control organized crime, there have been other national efforts aimed at assessing the activities of organized crime in the United States and providing recommendations for curbing its impact on society. Examples of advisory groups tasked with assessing the status of organized crime include the National Advisory Committee on Criminal Justice Standards and Goals (Organized Crime Task Force of 1976), the President's Commission on Organized Crime that met from 1983 through 1986, and the Organized Crime Council that met from 1970 to 1993. These groups have consistently concluded that organized crime remains a significant threat.

[30] Carrie Johnson, "Obama Team Faces Major Task in Justice Dept. Overhaul; Goal is to Restore Confidence in Law Enforcement Actions," *The Washington Post*, November 13, 2008, p. A02, Suburban Edition.

[31] U.S. Department of Justice, "Remarks prepared for delivery by Attorney General Michael B. Mukasey on International Organized Crime at the Center for Strategic and International

Studies," press release, April 23, 2008, http://www.usdoj.gov/ag/speeches/2008/ag-speech-080425.html.

[32] See the Department of Justice, Organized Crime and Racketeering Section website at http://www.usdoj.gov/criminal/links/ocrs.html.

[33] Because the FBI is the federal law enforcement agency leading the fight against organized crime, much of the discussion on federal crime control efforts in this report refers to the FBI. The examples used in this report, therefore, do not provide a comprehensive view of the federal efforts against organized crime.

[34] The FBI identifies organized crime threats on its website at *http://www.fbi.gov/hq/cid/orgcrime/aboutocs.htm.*

[35] From remarks by Chris Swecker, Acting Executive Assistant Director Law Enforcement Services, Federal Bureau of Investigation in U.S. Congress, House Committee on Homeland Security, Subcommittee on Management, Integration, and Oversight, *9/11 Reform Act: Examining the Implementation of the Human Smuggling and Trafficking Center*, 109th Cong., 2nd sess., March 8, 2006.

[36] While task forces tend to focus on investigating crimes, working groups tend to focus on discussing various threats and developing strategies to counter the threats.

[37] See the Federal Bureau of Investigation, Minneapolis Division Field Office website at http://minneapolis.fbi.gov/taskforces.htm#organized_crime.

[38] An example of one such task force is referenced in: Federal Bureau of Investigation, "Pedro D. Ruiz Named SAC of New York Field Office's Intelligence Division," press release, September 19, 2007, http://www.fbi.gov/pressrel/pressrel07/ruiz091707.htm.

[39] See the Department of Justice, Organized Crime and Racketeering Section website at http://www.usdoj.gov/criminal/links/ocrs.html.

[40] United Nations Office of Drugs and Crime, *United Nations Convention Against Transnational Organized Crime and the Protocols Thereto*, United Nations, New York, 2004.

[41] INTERPOL is the largest international police organization, composed of 187 member countries. It facilitates international law enforcement cooperation, primarily through maintaining secure global police communication systems, operating data services and databases for police, providing operational police support, and promoting police training and development. For more information on INTERPOL, see http://www.interpol.int/.

[42] The USNCB transmits, responds to, and executes requests for international law enforcement cooperation in which the United States is involved. For more information on the USNCB, see http://www.usdoj.gov/usncb/.

[43] From remarks by Grant D. Ashley, Assistant Director, Criminal Investigative Division, Federal Bureau of Investigation, in U.S. Congress, Senate Committee on Foreign Relations, *Combating Transnational Crime and Corruption in Europe*, 108th Cong., 1st sess., October 30, 2003.

[44] Department of Justice, Office of the Inspector General, Audit Division, *The External Effects of the Federal Bureau of Investigation's Reprioritization Efforts*, Audit Report 05-37, September 2005, p. 73.

[45] Ibid., p. 14.

[46] The specific number of agents allocated to and actually utilized on organized crime cases is not publically available after FY2004. For this reason, CRS is unable to determine the current relationship between agents allocated to and agents utilized on organized crime matters.

[47] U.S. Department of Justice, "Remarks prepared for delivery by Attorney General Michael B. Mukasey on International Organized Crime at the Center for Strategic and International Studies," press release, April 23, 2008, http://www.usdoj.gov/ag/speeches/2008/ag-speech-080425.html.

[48] Department of Justice, Office of the Inspector General, Audit Division, *The External Effects of the Federal Bureau of Investigation's Reprioritization Efforts*, Audit Report 05-37, September 2005, pp. 74-75.

[49] From remarks by Robert S. Mueller III, Director, Federal Bureau of Investigation, in U.S. Congress, Senate Committee on Appropriations, *Commerce, Justice, Science, and Related Appropriations for FY2008*, 110th Cong., 1st sess., April 26, 2007, p. 305.

[50] U.S. Department of Justice, Office of the Inspector General, Audit Division, *The External Effects of the Federal Bureau of Investigation's Reprioritization Efforts*, Audit Report 05-37, September 2005, pp. 73-75, http://www.usdoj.gov/oig/reports/FBI/a0537/final.pdf. CRS calculated the number of cases per agent based on the number of agents reported to be working on organized crime matters and the number of organized crime cases reportedly opened for FY2000 and FY2004.

[51] The specific number of agents working on organized crime cases is not publically available after FY2004. For this reason, CRS is unable to determine whether the workload of agents working organized crime cases has fluctuated from the FY2004 level.

[52] See the Bureau of Justice Statistics flowchart illustrating case flow through the criminal justice system at http://www.ojp.usdoj.gov/bjs/largechart.htm.

[53] Committee on Law and Justice, National Research Council, *Transnational Organized Crime: Summary of a Workshop*, ed. Peter Reuter and Carol Petrie (Washington: National Academy Press, 1999), pp. 1-2.

[54] As mentioned, drug trafficking organizations (DTOs) are considered by DOJ and the FBI as separate from organized crime groups. Although many organized crime groups are involved in drug smuggling, trafficking, and distribution— among various other crimes—DTOs' *primary* involvement is drugs. For more information on the U.S. policy and efforts to combat drug trafficking, see CRS Report RL32352, *War on Drugs: Reauthorization and Oversight of the Office of National Drug Control Policy*, by Mark Eddy.

[55] The FBI identifies organized crime threats on its website at *http://www.fbi.gov/hq/cid/orgcrime/aboutocs.htm.*

[56] For purposes of this discussion, the term *Russian organized crime* refers to both Russian and Eurasian crime groups operating in the United States. The FBI and other experts also reference the combination of Russian and Eurasian crime groups under an umbrella term. See, for example, James O. Finckenauer and Jay Albanese, "Organized Crime in North America," in *Handbook of Transnational Crime and Justice*, ed. Philip Reichel (Thousand Oaks, CA: Sage, 2005), pp. 439-456.).

[57] U.S. Congress, House Committee on International Relations, *Threat from International Organized Crime and Global Terrorism*, 105th Cong., 1st sess., October 1, 1997.

[58] Russian crime groups in Russia have a more hierarchical structure than those groups operating in the United States. These groups, such as the Vory V Zakone, or "thieves-in-law," exhibit a structure more similar to the Italian Cosa Nostra. See Alexander Sukharenko, "The Use of Corruption by 'Russian' Organized Crime in the United States," *Trends in Organized Crime*, vol. 8, no. 2 (Winter 2004), pp. 118-129. Also see James O. Finckenauer and Jay Albanese, "Organized Crime in North America," in *Handbook of Transnational Crime and Justice*, ed. Philip Reichel (Thousand Oaks, CA: Sage, 2005), pp. 439-456.

[59] From remarks by Grant D. Ashley, Assistant Director, Criminal Investigative Division, Federal Bureau of Investigation, in U.S. Congress, Senate Committee on Foreign Relations, *Combating Transnational Crime and Corruption in Europe*, 108th Cong., 1st sess., October 30, 2003.

[60] These are the cities in which the FBI has set up special investigative units dedicated to investigating Russian organized crime.

[61] Federal Bureau of Investigation, "Inside the FBI: Organized Crime," press release, February 13, 2009, http://www.fbi.gov/inside/archive/inside021309.htm.

[62] James O. Finckenauer and Jay Albanese, "Organized Crime in North America," in *Handbook of Transnational Crime and Justice*, ed. Philip Reichel (Thousand Oaks, CA: Sage, 2005), pp. 439-456.

[63] Federal Bureau of Investigation, "Testimony of Grant D. Ashley, Assistant Director, Criminal Investigative Division, FBI Before the Subcommittee on European Affairs, Committee on

Foreign Relations, United States Senate," press release, October 30, 2003, http://www.fbi.gov/congress/congress03/ashley103003.htm.

[64] Glenn E. Curtis, Seth L. Elan, and Rexford A. Hudson, et al., "Transnational Activities of Chinese Crime Organizations: A Report Prepared under an Interagency Agreement by the Federal Research Division, Library of Congress," *Trends in Organized Crime*, vol. 7, no. 3 (Spring 2002), pp. 19-57.

[65] Ko-Lin Chin, *Chinatown Gangs: Extortion, Enterprise, Ethnicity* (New York: Oxford University Press, 2000).

[66] Federal Bureau of Investigation, Organized Crime: Asian Criminal Enterprises, http://www.fbi.gov/hq/cid/orgcrime/asiancrim.htm.

[67] According to the FBI, there are four main Italian organized crime groups operating in the United States: the Sicilian Mafia (from which the LCN was formed), the Camorra or Neapolitan Mafia, the 'Ndrangheta or Calabrian Mafia, and the Sacra Corona Unita or United Sacred Crown. The term "Mafia" tends to be an encapsulating term referencing all of these groups.

[68] The five principal crime families that make up the LCN are the Bonanno, the Colombo, the Genovese, the Gambino, and the Luchese families.

[69] Other principal threats that the LCN poses to American society are labor racketeering, political corruption, extortion, theft, bribery, kidnapping, fraud, counterfeiting, infiltration of legitimate businesses, murders, and bombings.

[70] James O. Finckenauer, *La Cosa Nostra in the United States*, International Center, National Institute of Justice, 2007, http://www.docstoc.com/docs/416307/La-Cosa-Nostra-in-the-Unites-States---2000.

[71] Frank J. Marine, Organized Crime and Racketeering Section, United States Department of Justice, Washington, District of Columbia, USA, "The effects of organized crime on legitimate business," *Journal of Financial Crime*, vol. 13, no. 2 (2006), pp. 214-234.

[72] James B. Jacobs, Christopher Panarella, and Jay Worthington, *Busting the Mob: United States v. Cosa Nostra* (New York: New York University Press, 1994).

[73] John DiStasio, "International Organized Crime Center," *United States Attorneys' Bulletin*, vol. 51, no. 5 (September 2003), pp. 2-6.

[74] Clint Williamson, "Balkan Organized Crime: The Emerging Threat," *United States Attorneys' Bulletin*, vol. 51, no. 5 (September 2003), pp. 42-48.

[75] *World Encyclopedia of Organized Crime*, ed. Jay Robert Nash (Dallas: Zane Publishing, 1995).

[76] The Organized Crime Council includes leaders from nine federal law enforcement agencies: the Federal Bureau of Investigation; the U.S. Drug Enforcement Agency; the Bureau of Alcohol, Tobacco, Firearms and Explosives; the U.S. Immigration and Customs Enforcement; the U.S. Secret Service; the Internal Revenue Service; the U.S. Postal Inspection Service; Diplomatic Security; and the U.S. Department of Labor, Office of the Inspector General.

[77] Organized Crime Council, *Overview of the Law Enforcement Strategy to Combat International Organized Crime*, U.S. Department of Justice, April 2008. In this Strategy, the Organized Crime Council uses the broad term *international organized crime* to include organized crime in the United States. Former U.S. Attorney General Michael Mukasey has underscored the inclusion of domestic organized crime under the umbrella term of international organized crime, citing the globalization of crime and of groups with member around the world (including the United States). See U.S. Department of Justice, "Remarks Prepared for Delivery by Attorney General Michael B. Mukasey on International Organized Crime at the Center for Strategic and International Studies," April 23, 2008, http://www.usdoj.gov/ag/speeches/2008/ag_speech_080423.html.

[78] U.S. Department of Justice, "Remarks Prepared for Delivery by Attorney General Michael B. Mukasey on International Organized Crime at the Center for Strategic and International Studies," April 23, 2008, http://www.usdoj.gov/ag/speeches/2008/ag_speech_080423.html.

[79] Organized Crime Council, *Overview of the Law Enforcement Strategy to Combat International Organized Crime*, U.S. Department of Justice, April 2008, pp. 14-15.

[80] Money laundering is codified as a federal crime at 18 U.S.C. § 1956.

[81] See the Overview of Law Enforcement on the FinCEN website at http://www.fincen.gov/law_enforcement/.

[82] For more information on the money laundering discussions in Congress preceding the Money Laundering Control Act of 1986, see U.S. Congress, Senate Committee on the Judiciary, *Money Laundering Legislation*, Hearing on S. 572, S. 1335, and S. 1385, 99th Cong., 1st sess., October 29, 1985, S.Hrg. 99-540.

[83] "Supreme Court Narrows Scope of Money-Laundering Statute," *Criminal Justice Newsletter*, July 2008, pp. 1-3.

[84] U.S. Congressman Bobby Scott, "Prevent All Cigarette Trafficking Act of 2008," press release, September 9, 2008, http://www.bobbyscott.house.gov/index.php?option=com_content&task=view&id=346&Itemid=89.

[85] U.S. Government Accountability Office, *Intellectual Property: U.S. Efforts have Contributed to Strengthened Laws, but Significant Enforcement Challenges Remain*, GAO-05-788T, June 14, 2005, http://www.gao.gov/new.items/d05788t.pdf. Counterfeit and pirated goods are those that are either fake copies or copies that have been reproduced without authorization.

[86] From remarks by John C. Stedman, Lieutenant, Sheriff's Department, County of Los Angeles, before the U.S. Congress, Senate Committee on Homeland Security and Government Affairs, *Counterfeit Goods: Easy Cash for Criminals and Terrorists*, 109th Cong., 1st sess., May 25, 2005, p. 8. Intellectual property rights (IPR) include copyrights, trademarks, trade secrets, and patents.

[87] Office of the United States Trade Representative, *Anti-Counterfeiting Trade Agreement (ACTA)*, August 4, 2008, http://www.ustr.gov/assets/Document_Library/Fact_Sheets/2008/asset_upload_file760_15084.pdf?ht=.

[88] Todd Bullock, "Narcotics, Counterfeiting Help Fund North Korea, U.S. Says: Senate hearing discusses Pyongyang's criminal operations," *America.gov*, April 26, 2006, http://www.america.gov/st/washfile-english/2006/April/20060426135925tjkcollub0.8716699.html.

[89] Gregory F. Treverton, Carl Matthies, and Karla J. Cunningham, et al., *Film Piracy, Organized Crime, and Terrorism*, RAND Corporation, Safety and Justice Program and the Global Risk and Security Center, 2009, http://www.rand.org/pubs/monographs/2009/RAND_MG742.pdf.

[90] *Mapping the Global Structure*, National Intelligence Council, Report of the National Intelligence Council's 2020 Project, Based on consultations with nongovernmental experts around the world, Washington, D.C., December 2004, p. 96.

[91] Angela Veng Mei Leong, "Criminal Finance: Money Laundering and Terrorist Financing," in *The Disruption of International Organised Crime: An Analysis of Legal and Non-Legal Strategies* (Burlington, VT: Ashgate Publishing Company, 2007), pp. 29-67.

[92] Gregory F. Treverton, Carl Matthies, and Karla J. Cunningham, et al., *Film Piracy, Organized Crime, and Terrorism*, RAND Corporation, Safety and Justice Program and the Global Risk and Security Center, 2009, http://www.rand.org/pubs/monographs/2009/RAND_MG742.pdf.

[93] Pat Milton, "FBI Worries About an Osama-Sopranos Link," *Associated Press*, October 1, 2006, http://www.redorbit.com/news/general/676652/fbi_worries_about_an_osamasopranos_link/index.html.

[94] Organized Crime Council, *Overview of the Law Enforcement Strategy to Combat International Organized Crime*, U.S. Department of Justice, April 2008, p. 3.

[95] Ibid.

[96] U.S. General Accounting Office, *Combating Terrorism: Interagency Framework and Agency Programs to Address the Overseas Threat*, GAO-03-165, May 2003, *http://www.gao.gov/new.items/d03165.pdf.*

[97] From remarks by Robert S. Mueller III, Director, Federal Bureau of Investigation, in U.S. Congress, Senate Committee on Appropriations, *Commerce, Justice, Science, and Related Appropriations for FY2008*, 110th Cong., 1st sess., April 26, 2007, p. 305.

[98] From remarks by Bruce Swartz, Deputy Assistant Attorney General, Criminal Division, U.S. Department of Justice, at U.S. Congress, Senate Committee on Foreign Relations, *Hearing on Law Enforcement Treaties: Treaty Doc. 107-18, Inter-American Convention Against Terrorism; Treaty Doc. 108-6, Protocol of Amendment to the International Convention on the Simplification and Harmonization of Customs Procedures; Treaty Doc. 108-11, Council of Europe Convention on Cybercrime; Treaty Doc. 108-16, U.N. Convention Against Transnational Organized Crime and Protocols on Trafficking in Persons and Smuggling of Migrants*, 108th Cong., 2nd sess., June 17, 2004, pp. 29-37.

[99] Examples of international law enforcement partnerships can be found on the FBI's website at http://www.fbi.gov/hq/cid/orgcrime/lcnindex.htm#pantheon, http://www.fbi.gov/hq/cid/orgcrime/asiancrim.htm, and http://www.fbi.gov/page2/feb09/organizedcrime_021309.html.

[100] U. S . Department of Justice, *The Electronic Frontier: The Challenge of Unlawful Conduct Involving the Use of the Internet*, A Report of the President's Working Group on Unlawful Conduct on the Internet, March 2000, p. Appendix B, *http://www.usdoj.gov/criminal/cybercrime/append.htm#B.*

[101] See the Omnibus Diplomatic Security and Antiterrorism act of 1968, Title XII of P.L. 99-399. For more detailed information regarding the United States extraterritorial jurisdiction as well as the specific crimes are included in this jurisdiction, see CRS Report 94-166, *Extraterritorial Application of American Criminal Law*, by Charles Doyle.

[102] Thomas M. Sanderson, "Transnational Terror and Organized Crime: Blurring the Lines," *SAIS Review*, vol. XXIV, no. 1 (Winter-Spring 2004), pp. 49-61.

[103] *Mapping the Global Structure*, National Intelligence Council, Report of the National Intelligence Council's 2020 Project, Based on consultations with nongovernmental experts around the world, Washington, D.C., December 2004, p. 96.

[104] Louise Shelley, "The Globalization of Crime and Terrorism," *Global Issues*, February 2006, pp. 42-45.

[105] Ibid.

[106] Ibid.

[107] "Supreme Court Narrows Scope of Money-Laundering Statute," *Criminal Justice Newsletter*, July 2008, pp. 1-3.

In: Organized Crime in the U.S.
Editor: Wesley B. Knowles
ISBN: 978-1-60741-524-4

Chapter 2

IMPACT ON U.S. OF ASIAN TRANSNATIONAL CRIME

Asian Transnational Organized Crime

INTRODUCTION

By the late 20th century, organized criminal groups throughout the world were able to exploit the same economic liberalization, technology advances, and open borders that enabled multinational corporations to grow and prosper. Today, organized crime is a transnational phenomenon—and a cause for worldwide concern.

Transnational crime groups may have profited more from globalization than legitimate businesses, which are subject to domestic and host country laws and regulations. Transnational crime syndicates and networks, abetted by official corruption, blackmail, and intimidation, can use open markets and open societies to their full advantage.

As part of its effort to build an international research agenda that will help the United States better understand potential threats from transnational crime, the National Institute of Justice (NIJ) supported a project to preliminarily assess organized crime in eight Asian countries or administrative regions (Cambodia, China, Hong Kong, Japan, Macau, the Philippines, Taiwan, and Thailand); pinpoint research issues of mutual interest to U.S. and Asian researchers; identify potential research partners (and their affiliated institutions) in Asia who might work collaboratively on these issues; and locate indigenous data sources that would be accessible to U.S. investigators.

Definition of Terms

This study uses the definition of an organized crime group that was established by an ad hoc committee of United Nations member states working on a convention to facilitate the prevention and combating of transnational organized crime:

"A structured group of three or more persons existing for a period of time and acting in concert with the aim of committing one or more serious crimes or offen[s]es in order to obtain, directly or indirectly, a financial or other material benefit."

According to the convention, an offense is transnational if—

1. It is committed in more than one state.
2. It is committed in one state but a substantial part of its preparation, planning, direction, or control takes place in another state.
3. It is committed in one state but involves an organized criminal group that engages in criminal activities in more than one state.
4. It is committed in one state but has substantial effects in another state.

Study Methods

To achieve the multiple purposes of this project, researchers pursued several paths of inquiry:

- **Interviews.** On three separate visits to Asia—together comprising about 4 months—researchers interviewed people familiar with organized crime in that part of the world. Altogether, they interviewed 139 subjects, including 61 Asian law enforcement officials, 30 U.S. officials (e.g., Federal Bureau of Investigation legal attachés, Drug Enforce ment Administration representatives, immigration and customs officials, resident legal advisors for a U.S. embassy and consulate, and secret service personnel), 27 professors/researchers, 13 nongovernmental organization (NGO) workers, 6 persons engaged in commercial sex acts (i.e., prostitutes, exotic dancers, and other employees) or owners of sex establishments (such as brothels, sex clubs, and massage parlors), and 2 reporters. In addition, researchers spoke with law enforcement officials from the FBI and the U.S. Department of Justice's Organized Crime and Racketeering Section in Washington, D.C., who are dealing with organized crime matters and with staff in the Office to Monitor and Combat Trafficking in Persons at the U.S. Department of State.

- **Field visits.** Researchers participated in a police raid of a sex club in Taipei, visited a detention center for illegal immigrants outside Taipei (where they interviewed two young Chinese women detainees), talked extensively to local residents of a leading migrant-sending community in China, and toured some crime hot spots accompanied by other U.S. or local authorities.

- **Surveys.** Researchers asked a select number of experts in Beijing, Taipei, and Hong Kong to complete a survey instrument on organized crime in their respective jurisdictions and to prepare brief analyses on two illegal markets—drug trafficking and human smuggling and trafficking.

- **Collection and analyses of documents.** Researchers examined 11 indictments involving Asian crime groups in the United States and a large volume of both the English and Chinese literature on Asian organized crime. They also had unique access to the original data from two studies undertaken by Ko-lin Chin (one of this report's two investigators): a recently completed study on the social organization of human smuggling groups and an ongoing project on the drug trade in Southeast Asia's Golden Triangle. These two studies involved interviews with hundreds of human smugglers and drug growers, producers, and traffickers.

For the most part, this monograph focuses on the project's preliminary assessment and provides a framework for the issues associated with transnational organized crime in Asia. Interested readers may obtain the full report, which is available on the National Criminal Justice Reference Service Web site at www.ncjrs.org/ pdffiles1 /nij/grants/2 1331 0.pdf.

1. In the Eye of the Beholder: Perceptions of the Problem

What are the most serious problems associated with organized crime in the eight study sites? The answer to that question depends on who is asked. U.S. officials, whether in Asia or Washington, D.C., responded differently than Asian authorities, and even among the latter group, opinions varied according to jurisdiction.

The U.S. authorities who were contacted viewed several offenses (including drug, arms, and human trafficking) as serious problems that affect interests of the United States and undermine the stability of its Asian allies.

Asian respondents, broadly speaking, tended to view "traditional" organized crime activities (such as extortion, gambling, loan sharking, prostitution, debt collection, and violence) committed by local and regional groups as a higher priority than transnational crimes. The following section offers a brief countryby-country summary of the major organized crime issues and problems perceived by Asian authorities.

Asian Authorities' Perspective

Cambodia

The two leading organized crime problems in Cambodia are drug production/trafficking and human trafficking. Cambodian officials are concerned that drugs produced in neighboring countries are being trafficked into Cambodia for local consumption. Drug traffickers also use Cambodia as a transit country, but Cambodian authorities are less alarmed by this. The trafficking of Cambodian women into Thailand for sexual activities and the presence of a large number of Vietnamese women in Cambodia who are engaged in prostitution are major concerns for nongovernmental organizations (NGOs) in Asia. According to NGO representatives in Cambodia, however, local authorities are reluctant to crack down on the local commercial sex trade because they want to promote Cambodia as a place for cheap sex to attract tourists.[1] Some NGO personnel believe that Cambodian authorities are either directly involved in the sex trade or benefit from it. These same sources indicate that there is no link between terrorism and human trafficking in Cambodia.

China

For Chinese authorities, the gravest organized crime problems, in order of seriousness, are:[2]

- **Drug distribution.** The government is alarmed by the dramatic increase in the number of heroin addicts in China, and authorities believe that local and foreign-based drug syndicates are importing heroin from the neighboring Golden Triangle area and distributing it throughout the country (see "Drug Production and Trafficking in the Golden Triangle").
- **Gambling and prostitution.** After being nearly eradicated following the 1949 communist takeover in China, gambling and prostitution are now thriving.
- **Violence.** Crime groups are becoming better armed and more violent, and Chinese authorities are concerned about violent acts committed by mobsters against rival gang members, ordinary citizens, business owners, and government authorities.

As for the future, according to Chen Xiao-cun of the Criminal Investigation Division, Ministry of Public Security, even more serious problems may lie ahead:

> Our main concerns are that: (1) organizations with an underworld nature will penetrate into the legitimate business sector, (2) gangsters will get involved in politics and run for public office, and (3) they will eventually hook up with foreign-based organized crime groups.

Evidence suggests that many crime groups in China have already monopolized certain wholesale businesses and that the majority of these groups are protected by local authorities known as baohusan, or "protecting umbrella." In general, official corruption is seen to be a large and growing problem in China. Organized crime is a municipal, local, or regional (rather than national or transnational) phenomenon. Given the pace of economic development in China, and the interest of external investors in this development, the involvement of criminal organizations has significant implications, including a potential chilling effect on economic growth.

DRUG PRODUCTION AND TRAFFICKING IN THE GOLDEN TRIANGLE

The focal point of illicit drug production and trafficking in Southeast Asia is known as the Golden Triangle, a rugged, mountainous region that overlaps the borders of Burma (Myanmar), Laos, and Thailand. Although the tri-border region accounts for the majority of heroin production in Southeast Asia, the amount of heroin produced in the area has decreased by approximately 70 percent in the past 5 years. In 2004, Burma and Laos accounted for nearly all heroin produced in the region. Eradication efforts and the enforcement of poppy-free zones have combined to depress cultivation levels.

However, the decline in heroin production is being offset by an increase in the production of amphetamine-type stimulants (ATS). Methamphetamine is cheaper and easier to produce than heroin; it entails a simple process that starts with ephedrine, the principal alkaloid of ephedra, a shrub that grows wild on vast expanses of the nearby Chinese province of Yunnan.

Much of the heroin produced in the Golden Triangle reaches markets through southern China, although increased law enforcement pressure by Chinese authorities has forced some traffickers to seek new routes through Thailand. In Laos, the Mekong River is a major conduit for heroin trafficking and is patrolled in only a few areas. Many key drug areas, particularly in the north, are virtually inaccessible to Laotian officials. According to Interpol, "ethnic Chinese traffickers control the heroin trade in Oceania (often with Vietnamese criminal organizations), Malaysia, and the few remaining markets in Canada and the United States."

Hong Kong's position as a key port city and its proximity to the Golden Triangle and mainland China have made it a natural transit point for heroin moving from Southeast Asia to global markets. Although the amount of heroin transiting through Hong Kong appears to be diminishing, drug traffickers continue to use it as a base of operations.

Tens of thousands of Chinese men and women are smuggled abroad each year to be laborers or to be sexually exploited. The arrival of large numbers of undocumented Chinese persons for these purposes is a cause of major concern in many countries.[3] Nonetheless, Chinese authorities do not consider this to be an organized crime problem—or even a Chinese problem, because most snakeheads (human smugglers) are Chinese-Americans.[4] Local authorities noted the many benefits of having large numbers of their own people working abroad and sending money home. Indeed, study researchers observed considerable new housing development that is being fueled by money allegedly sent home by illegal workers in the United States.

Hong Kong

Hong Kong was a British colony for more than 100 years before it returned to Chinese control in 1997. It is now a special administrative region—meaning that it has a degree of autonomy— although that status is in constant contention with the mainland. Hong Kong has long been home to the secretive, ritualistic criminal organizations known as triads.[5] Authorities have a strong history of combating these triads—and of battling corruption as well—and the jurisdiction is widely known for its sophisticated and wellresourced police operations.[6] At the same time, Hong Kong is subject to much illicit movement of goods, services, and people to and from the mainland. U.S. Drug Enforcement Administration (DEA) representatives in Hong Kong reported that some 18 million tons of cargo (both legal and illegal) destined for the United States pass through the port of Hong Kong in a year—a situation that clearly poses a security concern for the United States.

According to the elite Organized Crime and Triad Bureau (OCTB) of the Hong Kong Police, the leading organized crime problems in Hong Kong are car theft and smuggling, human smuggling, cross-border organized crime involving China and Macau, money laundering, drug trafficking, debt collection, and triad monopolies. Triad societies control private bus routes, fish markets, street markets, wholesale markets, entertainment centers, parking services, prostitution, illegal gambling, and extortion. In addition, each of the three triads (the Wo Shing Wo, the San Yee On, and the 14K) is said to be involved in the manufacture and street- level distribution of pirated VCDs and DVDs.

As a major transportation and financial center of Asia and a transit point in and out of China, Hong Kong has been a hub for transnational organized crime activities for the past 30 years. Although triad organizations are active in Hong Kong, the OCTB indicated that no international triad organization exists. DEA representatives in Hong Kong said that drug trafficking was not well organized at the wholesale level. Instead, small groups of individual entrepreneurs serve as wholesalers, and the triads are mostly involved in organizing the street-level retail drug business.

Authorities interviewed said that the triads "are not interested in involving themselves in politics." The kinds of political/ideological missions associated with terrorism are said to be outside the ambitions or interests of the Hong Kong triads.

Japan

In Japan, the most serious organized crime problems are almost always related to the notorious Japanese organized crime groups—the yakuza.[7] Japanese authorities are mostly concerned with yakuza involvement in gambling, prostitution, amphetamine trafficking, and the victimization of legitimate businesses. According to Chief Seijirou Ikegami of the Anti-Organized Crime Division, Ueno Police Department, Tokyo Metropolitan Police, Japanese officials are also alarmed by the presence of a large number of legal and illegal immigrants from China (mostly Shanghainese, Fujianese, and Northeasterners) who are involved in organized crime activities and considered to be heavily armed and dangerous.

Because of its wealth and the spending power of Japanese businessmen, Japan has become a major destination country for women from Thailand, the Philippines, Colombia, China, Korea, and several other countries. In addition to women from abroad, Japan has a large number of local Japanese women who are involved in the sex industry.[8] Japanese authorities are convinced that yakuza members are heavily involved in the transportation and control of foreign persons for sexual purposes, but they do not view this as their most serious organized crime problem because (1) they believe these persons are not being forced into their activities, and (2) the Japanese public has not pressured authorities to do something about it.

Macau

Macau, a former Portuguese colony, is, like Hong Kong, a special administrative region of China. Macau aspires to be a tourist mecca and is dominated by gambling casinos, prostitution, and drugs. According to Sio-chak Wong, director of the Judiciary Police of Macau, the two major organized crime problems in Macau are gambling and illegal immigration/prostitution. Gambling is dominated by triad groups transplanted from Hong Kong, while illegal immigration/prostitution is controlled by crime groups formed by mainland Chinese. Recently, these Chinese crime groups began to be involved in fraud, money laundering, and the smuggling of stolen goods from Macau to China.

Because the Macau administration relies heavily on taxes from gambling—and prostitution is considered to be an important adjunct to the gambling industry—Macau authorities are reluctant to crack down on crime groups involved in these activities. As a result, organized crime groups maintain a strong presence in the gambling business in Macau. At the same time, Macau's commercial sex establishments are booming because of the arrival of large numbers of prostitutes from China.

The Philippines

Because of political instability and corruption, the country's economy is in disarray, which results in large numbers ofFilipino people having to go overseas to work. Many of them are women, and a significant percentage of these women leave with an "entertainer visa" and end up being sexually exploited abroad.[9] Although the Philippine government has recently passed an anti-trafficking law, few human traffickers have ever been prosecuted and punished (see "Trafficking in Persons Report"). But Filipino officials are less concerned with the problem of Filipino persons engaged in prostitution abroad than with high-profile crimes such as drug trafficking, kidnapping for ransom, hijacking, bank robbery, prostitution, illegal gambling, and firearms smuggling.

The trafficking of amphetamine (called shabu in the Philippines) from China to the Philippines has been a major concern of Filipino authorities for a long time. Recently, many shabu laboratories have been established in the Philippines, in part because of the improved effectiveness of tighter coastal patrols in stopping the drug flow from abroad. Authorities indicated that the drug business in the Philippines is controlled by predominantly Filipino-Chinese, or Chinese from China, Hong Kong, and Taiwan who are protected by local politicians.

Trafficking in Persons Report

The International Labour Organization (ILO)— the United Nations agency charged with addressing labor standards, employment, and social protection issues—estimates that 12.3 million people throughout the world are enslaved in forced labor, bonded labor, sexual servitude, and involuntary servitude at any given time. Millions of these victims are trafficked within their own national borders. According to the State Department's 2005 *Trafficking in Persons (TIP) Report,* approximately 600,000 to 800,000 men, women, and children are trafficked across international borders each year; of these, about 80 percent are female, and up to half are minors. The majority of transnational victims are trafficked into commercial sexual exploitation.

Tier Ranking System

The *TIP Report* evaluates the performance of 150 countries in terms of their compliance with the minimum standards of the Trafficking Victims Protection Act (TVPA) of 2000 (reauthorized in 2003 and 2005). Tier 1 countries are deemed to be in full compliance. Tier 2 countries are not in compliance but are making significant efforts to become so. Tier 3 countries are not compliant and are not making significant efforts toward that end. A Tier 3 assessment could trigger the withholding of certain types of U.S. aid.

The 2003 reauthorization of the TVPA created a Tier 2 Watch List of countries that warrant special scrutiny. The list consists of countries whose rating changed from the previous year's *TIP Report* or countries listed as Tier 2 in the current report where—

- The absolute number of victims of severe forms of trafficking is very significant or significantly increasing.
- There is a failure to provide evidence of increasing efforts to combat severe forms of human trafficking from the previous year— including increased investigations, prosecutions, and convictions of trafficking crimes; increased assistance to victims; and decreasing evidence of complicity by government officials.
- The determination that a country is making significant efforts to bring itself into compliance with minimum standards was based on commitments by the country to take additional future steps over the next year.

Since trafficking likely extends to every country in the world, the omission of a country from the *TIP Report* may only indicate a lack of adequate information.

The TVPA defines severe forms of trafficking as "(1) sex trafficking in which a commercial sex act is induced by force, fraud, or coercion, or in which the person induced to perform such an act has not attained 18 years of age; or (2) the recruitment, harboring, transportation, provision, or obtaining of a person for labor or services, through the use of force, fraud, or coercion for the purpose of subjection to involuntary servitude, peonage, debt bondage, or slavery."

Status of the Eight Sites in This Report

Of the eight sites that researchers visited, only Hong Kong was considered fully compliant with the minimum requirements of the Trafficking Victims Protection Act of 2000. Japan, Taiwan, and Thailand were assigned Tier 2 rankings, and Macau (due to insufficient information) was not listed at all.

Two countries—China and the Philippines— were put on the Tier 2 Watch List. In the case of China, this designation is due to its failure to provide evidence of increasing efforts to combat trafficking (specifically, its inadequate protection for trafficking victims—especially foreign women and Chinese women deported from Taiwan). The Philippines was placed on the watch list because, despite widespread allegations of law enforcement complicity in trafficking, the Government reported no prosecutions of trafficking-related corruption. The Government made "modestly better efforts" during the performance period to implement its 2003 anti-trafficking law, i.e., it dedicated four state prosecutors to focus on trafficking- related cases and provided training to law enforcement officials. The 2005 *TIP Report* indicates that "28 cases are currently under investigation" and that "at least 15 cases are being prosecuted under the anti-trafficking law and other statutes . . . . [But] corruption and a weak judiciary remain serious impediments to the effective prosecution of traffickers."

Cambodia, a source, destination, and transit country for men, women, and children trafficked for the purposes of sexual exploitation and forced labor, was assessed as Tier 3 for its lack of progress in combating severe forms of trafficking, particularly its failure to convict traffickers and public officials involved in trafficking. In addition, the Government failed to take effective action during the performance period to ensure that those responsible for a raid on an NGO shelter for trafficking victims (which included removal of several victims) were held accountable and brought to justice. In short, Cambodia's anti-trafficking efforts remained hampered by systemic corruption and an ineffectual judicial system.

TIP Report Assessment of Eight Countries

Country	Tier 1	Tier 2	Tier 2 Watch List	Tier 3	Inadequate Information
Cambodia				X	
China			X		
Hong Kong	X				
Japan		X			
Macau					X
Philippines			X		
Taiwan		X			
Thailand		X			

A U.S. Government official interviewed in Manila said that organized crime and terrorism in the Philippines are separate activities. The terrorists are said to be isolated groups and not involved in such transnational crimes as human trafficking and drug smuggling. A Filipino official indicated that some terrorist groups may be involved in kidnapping for ransom, but they do not play a major role in such crimes because their numbers are not strong in Manila, where most of the wealthy Chinese (who are potential victims) live.

Taiwan

In Taiwan, the number one organized crime problem is heijin, the penetration of mobsters into the legitimatebusiness sector and the political arena.[10] Many influential gangsters in Taiwan are now chief executive officers of major business conglomerates, and they are heavily involved in the businesses of bid-rigging, waste disposal, construction, cable television networks, telecommunications, stock trading, and entertainment. Further, starting in the mid-1980s, many criminals have successfully run for public office in order to protect themselves from police crackdowns.

In addition to heijin, Taiwanese authorities are concerned with traditional organized crime activities such as gambling, prostitution, loan sharking, debt collection, extortion, and gang violence. Kidnapping for ransom is also a serious concern; influential and wealthy figures are often targeted and, as a result, a large number of Taiwanese entrepreneurs have departed for a safe haven abroad.

A relatively recent and growing transnational crime problem is the production and distribution of pirated CDs and DVDs. Each of the three major criminal gangs surveyed in Taiwan is said to be involved in this business. Another transnational crime—drug trafficking—was cited as a problem but considered less worrisome to authorities than human smuggling. Even though Taiwan is a destination country for heroin from the Golden Triangle and amphetamine from China, Taiwanese authorities are more concerned with the influx of pros titutes (or potential prostitutes) from China, who are smuggled into Taiwan by boats across the Taiwan Strait or arrive through fraudulent marriages with Taiwanese citizens.[11]

At the time of this study, one detention facility was holding more than 1,000, mostly young, Chinese women awaiting deportation back to mainland China, some for as long as 9 months. Taiwanese law enforcement authorities were frustrated by dealing with uncooperative Chinese authorities on this issue. Also frustrating them were rulings of Taiwanese judges who do not consider human trafficking to be an organized crime problem and thus do not apply the country's anti-organized crime laws to the networks engaged in these activities.

As in mainland China, respondents in Taiwan reported no concerns about any possible connections between organized crime groups and either terrorist groups or so-called armed opposition groups.

Thailand

The two leading organized crime groups in Thailand are the jao phor (godfathers) and the United Wa State Army (or the Red Wa).[12] Jao phor are mostly ethnic Chinese based in the provinces who have business interests in both legitimate and criminal activities. Moreover, they have groups of associates and followers; move closely with powerful bureaucrats, policemen, and military figures; sit in positions in local administration; and play a key role in parliamentary elections. According to Thai authorities, jao phor groups reside in 39 of Thailand's 76 provinces. The United Wa State Army is also a major concern for the Thai government because this organization, located in the Burmese part of the Golden Triangle, is believed to be responsible for manufacturing and trafficking millions of methamphetamine tablets (called yaba or mad drug in Thailand) into the country for local consumption. Although heroin produced by the Red Wa and other groups in the Golden Triangle continues to pass through Thailand, Thai authorities are less concerned with this drug because the country's local heroin market is relatively small.

Thailand is also a source, transit, and destination country for trafficked women,[13] but Thai officials are not concerned by the sizeable presence of Burmese women engaged in prostitution in their country or by the trafficking of Thai women to Japan and Europe to be sexually exploited. Because prostitution is vital to the country's enormous tourist industry and Thai policemen are believed to be heavily bribed by sex establishment owners, authorities do not consider the illegal sex industry to be an organized crime problem.

U.S. Authorities' Viewpoint

As already noted, U.S. authorities are much more likely than their Asian counterparts to consider trans-national organized crime activities to be the more serious organized crime problems in Asia. This could be explained by differing focuses of the two groups, or might be attributable in some cases to lack of knowledge and understanding of the local situation by the Americans as a result of having to depend on outside sources for information. In any event, from the U.S. viewpoint, the problems of drug production and trafficking, human smuggling, trafficking in women and children for the purpose of prostitution, arms trafficking, and money laundering are all very serious problems in Asia. Americans interviewed also thought these activities have either a direct or indirect impact on U.S. interests or, at the very least, that they have undermined the stability and well-being of ally countries in Asia.

None of the Americans interviewed believes that terrorist groups and transnational organized crime groups are linked. (As previously indicated, this is the view held by some of the Asian authorities as well, among those who expressed any opinion on the issue.)

Researchers' Vantage Point

Contrary to the opinions of many in U.S. law enforcement, this study found that the relationship between traditional organized crime groups (such as the triads and the yakuza) and trans- national crime is tenuous. Asian authorities in China and Hong Kong indicated that human smuggling, for example, is carried out primarily by loose networks or "mom and pop" groups with no ties to organized crime—a claim borne out by data from personal interviews with such smugglers. This difference in understanding about who is engaged in transnational crime may account for some of the disparity in priorities between criminal justice agencies in the East and West. Another difficulty has to do with what constitutes transnational crime. As discussed earlier, Asian authorities may be reluctant to treat certain transnational activities as crime because they are beneficial to the local economy, and the people who are involved may not be gangsters or professional criminals. Such perceptual and communication problems pose challenges for collaborative research but are not insurmountable.

Based on the interviews, fieldwork, and literature review conducted as part of this project, the five leading organized crime problems in Asia (not necessarily ranked in the order presented here) are (1) drug production and trafficking, (2) trafficking in women and children, (3) human smuggling, (4) the links among organized crime/ politics/official corruption, and (5) the penetration of organized crime into legitimate businesses. For research purposes, it is recommended that funding be targeted to the first three problems (detailed below) because of the inevitable obstacles that U.S. researchers would face in trying to study criminal infiltration into politics and business—areas that, in any event, do not affect the United States directly. It is further recommended that research efforts be both bilateral (principally with China) and multilateral in nature. The full report identifies a wide variety of potentially will ing research partners and assesses their strengths and weaknesses.

- **Drug production and trafficking.** Traffickers are taking advantage of China's open-door policy and using the land route from the Golden Triangle to distribute heroin both to markets inside China and to ports where it can be shipped to other countries. This enables them to move hundreds of kilograms in one delivery and helps them develop a huge market as they wend their way through a country with more than 1.3 billion people. In addition, large quan tities of this heroin may reach the United States.
  Massive quantities of meth-amphetamine produced in the Golden Triangle are trafficked to Thailand. The explosion of methamphetamine use in Thailand has caused a serious internal problem and also exacerbated existing hostility between Thailand and Burma, thus worsening a volatile international situation. Amphetamine production in China has caused a problem of its use

there, and trafficking of amphetamine to Taiwan, Japan, and the Philippines has created problems for those countries.

- **Trafficking in women and children.** This human rights problem, which affects many thousands of victims, is getting worse rather than better. Research is needed to differentiate between trafficking and smuggling, and their respective consequences, to put to rest claims made by Asian law enforcement that women cross borders voluntarily to increase their income, and to remove the emotionalism surrounding this issue—as reflected in terms such as "sex slave" and "debt bondage."
- **Human smuggling.** In some ways, this is a more serious problem than human trafficking because of the numbers involved (millions, not thousands). In addition, smuggling fees per person have increased from about $30,000 in the early 1990s to $65,000 after the events of September 11, 2001. Smuggling has a direct impact on the United States because many illegal aliens end up in America.

2. Scope and Patterns of Organized Crime

Many crime groups exist in Asia, some of them indigenous and others imported from abroad or formed by foreigners. As with the task of ranking the seriousness of organized crime problems in Asia, an attempt to generalize the scope of each and every organized crime group is difficult because this may depend on the country, the group, and the product or service involved.

Scope

In general, most traditional organized crime groups (i.e., mafia-like criminal organizations in China, organized gangs in Taiwan, triad societies in Hong Kong and Macau, and jao phor in Thailand) are local in scope. Three Chinese organized crime syndicates identified in a recent U.N. study—the Liu Yong Syndicate, the Zhang Wei Syndicate, and the Liang Xiao Min Syndicate—were all said to be local or at most regional in their scope, and to be without cooperative relationships with other organized crime groups.[14]

No doubt, some members of such local/regional organizations may have influence at the national level, but their legal and illegal operations are more likely to be local in nature. An exception is the yakuza in Japan. A Japanese official said in an interview that yakuza members are very much involved in the trafficking of persons and the operation of sex establishments in Japan, and some members of these various crime groups may also travel to other countries or may be involved in bilateral or multinational criminal activities. However, they, and the members of other Asia-based organized crime groups, are not key players in trans- national criminal activities.[15]

A Chinese official in Beijing (referring to mafia-like crime groups known in China as "black societies") explained the organized crime/ transnational crime connection this way: "According to our law, there are four types of organized crime groups: (1) criminal groups; (2) criminal organizations; (3) black society-like criminal organizations; and (4) black societies. At this point, we don't yet have black societies, but we expect them to be formed in the very near future. The [other] above-mentioned three groups are not involved in transnational crime. That is because these groups are all territorial—their spheres of influence and their activities are restricted to their own turfs. They are not mature enough to establish a trans- national crime network." Similarly, assessments of specific criminal organizations in Taiwan do not indicate any involvement on the part of these groups in transnational crime. A drug market analysis in Taiwan, however, showed that some organized crime groups may be active in the transnational trafficking of new, synthetic drugs.

In the Philippines, interview participants said specifically that the transnational "headhunters" who recruit people for prostitution there are not members of organized crime groups. And, a Thai official stated: "In Thailand, there are influential groups [organized crime groups] and there are transnational organized groups formed by foreigners.

There is not much relationship existing between the influential groups and the transnational organized crime groups."

Even those nontraditional organized crime groups that are heavily involved in transnational crimes such as drug trafficking and human smuggling/trafficking are local or at most national in scope. Their transnational criminal operations are almost always compartmentalized. Most large-scale transnational criminal activities, such as the trafficking of hundreds of kilograms of heroin or the smuggling of hundreds of illegal immigrants, involve numerous independent groups operating in source, transit, and destination countries. There are also, however, "mom and pop," small-scale transnational criminal activities involving, for example, a couple trying to smuggle a small amount of drugs or two or three migrants from one country to another. What is unique about transnational crime is that it can be carried out in some cases by an individual (e.g., computer crime) or by a group or network with hundreds of members or associates.[16]

Specialization

Most of the study subjects suggested that there is little specialization among traditional organized crime groups. Most of these groups are involved in a variety of both legitimate and illegitimate businesses. While these crime groups continue to be involved in traditional organized crime activities such as gambling, prostitution, drug distribution, loan sharking, debt collection, and violence, they are also expanding their influence into legitimate businesses such as the stock market, construction, waste disposal, wholesale markets, and the food industry.

However, according to the study subjects, transnational crime networks are highly specialized. It is relatively unlikely for a human smuggling organization to be involved in drug trafficking, or for a drug-manufacturing group to participate in the trafficking of women for prostitution.

The only overlapping or non-specialization that may occur is among offenders who are involved in transportation. In this instance, individual members, as opposed to crime groups as a whole, may cross over in providing services for smuggling and trafficking. Even though different groups operate each transnational criminal activity in the source and destination countries, and these various groups do not get involved in more than one type of transnational crime, the same group responsible for transportation (e.g., a boat captain and crew) may simultaneously be involved in smuggling both drugs and human beings.

Structure or Opportunity?

Traditional organized crime groups are longstanding, preexisting groups, while transnational crime networks are developed in response to current criminal opportunities. Some of the traditional organized crime groups mentioned above have been in existence in Asia for centuries and they are most likely to continue to exist. These groups have names, structure, territory, and a strong attachment to their environment, and as a result are handicapped in taking advantage of criminal opportunities that are transnational in nature.[17] The second group, the networks of transnational crime, are more likely to emerge around specific opportunities. Very often, a nuclear or an extended family will initiate an operation in response to a new opportunity and people from the same village or at least the same ethnic group who are living in source, transit, and destination countries will be recruited to participate as members of a network that may dissolve after the criminal operation is successfully carried out.

This distinction has implications for both research and policy. For research, there is a need to expand the current thinking about the causes of organized crime and about the risks and vulnerabilities that may lead to the creation of criminal markets. There is also a need to better understand how those criminal markets operate in order to provide useful information to shape strategies and tactics to disrupt them. For policy, law enforcement officials need to do more thinking "out of the box" of tradition al, mafia-like structures in order to effectively combat the crime networks that are dominating transnational organized crime.

The Flow

There are several major movement patterns involving people who are sexually exploited, drugs, and laborers on the transnational scene.

Prostitutes. In Asia, the most notable flows of trafficked women are (1) from the Philippines to Japan, (2) from Thailand to Japan, (3) from Burma (Myanmar) to Thailand, (4) from Vietnam to Cambodia, and (5) from Nepal to India. There are also somewhat less notable movements such as (1) from Cambodia to Thailand, (2) from Laos to Thailand, and (3) from the Philippines to Korea.

The most significant development in human smuggling and trafficking, however, is the massive movement of women from China to other Asian countries and, indeed, to the rest of the world. Authorities in all the countries visited indicated that many Chinese women are showing up in their sex industries; sex establishments in Hong Kong, Taiwan, Macau, and Japan have almost been taken over by Chinese women. The presence of large numbers of Chinese women in the sex industries of Burma, Thailand, Singapore, Malaysia, Indonesia, Australia, and the United States has also been heavily reported.

Drugs. In Asia, heroin is produced in the Burmese part of the Golden Triangle and flows into the international market via either Thailand or China. China's heroin market is expanding rapidly, and heroin markets exist in most Southeast Asian countries and also in Australia. Methamphetamine also is produced in the Burmese part of the Golden Triangle; Thailand is the main market for the drug. It is smuggled into Thailand either across the Burma-Thai border or through Laos and Cambodia. Amphetamine is mainly produced in

China and smuggled into Taiwan, Japan, the Philippines, and other Asian countries.

Undocumented workers. A large number of Chinese laborers are smuggled by boat into Taiwan across the Taiwan Strait. Chinese are also arriving in Japan and Burma in large numbers. The presence of a substantial number of Chinese, both legal and illegal migrants, is a matter of concern for the majority of nations in Asia. Undocumented workers are also a matter of concern in the United States.

3. Impact on the United States

The following discussion does not deal with the garden variety of crimes that just happen to have been committed in the United States by Asians, nor the Asian street gangs that operate in certain U.S. cities. Instead, the focus is on those crimes that appear to be transnational in nature—the United States being on the receiving end—and that originate in (or at least involve) any of the eight countries (or administrative regions) that were the focal point of the study.

Further, impact and harm are construed broadly here, to include not only direct criminal activities in the United States, but also harm and/or potential harm to U.S. interests both at home and abroad. For example, given the history and the volatility of relations between mainland China and Taiwan, and the strong U.S. interest and investment in that area, criminal developments involving those entities are of critical interest to the United States. In other cases, where there are developing U.S. business interests, such as in China and in the casino industry in Macau, again there is the potential for a criminal impact on U.S. interests.

Additionally, a word about methodology is necessary. As noted, principal respondents in the interviews were nationals (scholars, law enforcement officials, and in some cases victims) of the respective countries that were visited. Thus, their perspectives of how what they know might impact the United States are pretty much speculative. Even in the cases of the U.S. officials that were interviewed in each country, their perspectives on the crime and organized crime problems are an "in country" view, albeit keeping U.S. interests very much in mind.

In addition to the interviews and field visits that were conducted, local scholars in Hong Kong and Taiwan prepared market assessments of the criminal markets of human trafficking and drug trafficking and analyses of the major organized crime groups in each of their respective areas. It should be recognized that these reflect the perspectives of the native scholars.

None of this should be construed to mean that the inter views, assessments, and analyses are not valuable—quite to the contrary. The original sources provided a foundation, a stepping-off point, to compare and relate what was learned from them with a plethora of existing secondary materials. The latter include in particular:

- The U.S. State Department's *Trafficking in Persons (TIP) Report* for 2004.
- "Sex Trafficking of Women in the United States" (a 2001 report to NIJ by Janice Raymond and Donna Hughes).[18]
- "The Commercial Sexual Exploitation of Children in the U.S., Canada, and Mexico" (a 2002 report to NIJ by Richard Estes and Neil Weiner).[19]
- "Survey of Practitioners to Assess the Local Impact of Transnational Crime" (a 2003 report to NIJ by Abt Associates).[20]
- *Blood Brothers: The Criminal Underworld of Asia* by Bertil Lintner (2002).[21]

Threat, Impact, and Harm to the United States

When asked about transnational crime, only a few of the Asian respondents referred to specific crimes impacting the United States. For example, according to members of the faculty of the Fuzhou Police College in China, the principal forms of transnational crime involving China and the United States are kidnapping and human trafficking. Officials of the Bureau of Investigation of the Ministry of Justice of Taiwan stated that fake IDs are used to gain Taiwanese passports for travel to the United States by Chinese who are being smuggled here. But these are not seen as high priority (or even medium priority for the most part) problems in Asia. On the other hand, human trafficking and smuggling were indeed high-priority issues for most of the U.S. authorities interviewed. These included U.S. officials both in Washington and abroad. For instance, an FBI official indicated that such activities as trafficking in women/children who are sexually exploited, trafficking in human beings for the purpose of labor, and illegal mmigration were transnational criminal activities of Chinese organized crime groups in the United States.

Human trafficking is one problem for which there is a seemingly vast difference in priority and perspective between Asian and U.S. authorities. The Asian authorities view what is happening in the transnational movement of people as mostly smuggling. People wanting to leave China, for example, pay smugglers to transport them to Taiwan or even to the United States. There is little or no coercion or deception in these cases. This is part of the reason for the Asian authorities' lack of concern.

The Asian experts interviewed also do not see this smuggling as an activity of traditional organized crime groups. A top criminal investigator with the Ministry of Public Security in Beijing told researchers that human trafficking was indeed "organized," but that it was not a form of organized crime. He indicated the main destination countries for Chinese women were Japan, Korea, Russia, Taiwan, and Hong Kong. A correspondent in Hong Kong indicated that none of the three most prom inent organized crime groups in Hong Kong (the San Yee On, the Wo Shing Wo, and the 14K) are involved in human smuggling or human trafficking. Other authorities in Hong Kong likewise said that there is very limited trafficking in Hong Kong, that the vast majority of people moving transnationally are smuggled (not trafficked), and that this is a "mom and pop" industry not controlled by organized crime. These views reflect those of authorities in the other locations visited as well. For example, representatives of the National Police Administration in Taiwan said there is no evidence of human smugglers engaging in other trans-national organized crime activities, nor are they involved with well-established organized crime groups. In fact, as previously noted, because the judges in Taiwan do not consider human smuggling to be an activity of organized crime, they do not enforce the Organized Crime Prevention Law against smugglers.

So what is the impact of Asian human smuggling/ trafficking on the United States? Both the United Nations and the United States (in the Department of State's annual *TIP Report*) make much of the connection between organized crime and human trafficking. The 2004 *TIP Report* concludes that trafficking fuels organized crime. As indicated above, interviews conducted for this study and examina-tion of the data from the *TIP Reports* seem to belie that claim—at least as far as the specific problem of smuggling/ trafficking from Asia to the United States is concerned.

Some empirical evidence sheds light on the issue. The Raymond and Hughes study[22] tracked incidents of trafficking to the United States between 1990 and 2000. Of 38 specific cases they described, 18 had an Asian connection, particularly from Thailand or elsewhere in Southeast Asia. From the brief descriptions of these cases, some are clearly alleged to have organized crime involvement, but a dozen or so cases over a 10-year period does not seem to be a very large number. Further, Raymond and Hughes's interview respon-dents in the 2001 study indicated that the trafficking organizations with which they were familiar were mostly small, having only one to five people involved. This supports a "mom and pop" characterization rather than one of organized crime.

So what does a typical mom-and-pop case look like? The "News Item" is illustrative. The Estes and Weiner study[23] surveyed a variety of sources, including 1,000 informants in 17 U.S. cities, in an examination of the commercial sexual exploitation of children (including trafficking). The study concluded that among the "less common" forms of this exploitation was participation by international organized crime networks. Only 10 percent of the children they encountered had been trafficked internationally, and that included from allsources (Africa, Central and Latin America, and Central and Eastern Europe) not just from Asia. Thus again, these findings do not support a belief that human trafficking to the United States by Asian organized crime is a major problem.

NEWS ITEM

U.S. Federal authorities arrested in Miami a husband and wife team who allegedly smuggled thousands of Chinese illegal immigrants into the United States over the past 20 years. Alexandre Wei, a Taiwanese national with French citizenship, and his wife Bing Xei, a Chinese citizen, used Miami, Florida, as the U.S. entry point for their clients, who usually ended their round-theworld journey in New York City. In Manila, U.S. and Philippine authorities arrested the couple's son Jacques, a suspected co-conspirator, along with six other Chinese. This family of people smugglers would first send their clients from China to the Philippines and several other Asian countries. They would then be moved to France, Suriname, or the French territories in the Caribbean, Jamaica, or the Bahamas. From the West Indies, the illegal immigrants were moved to Florida. The illegal immigrants were charged as much as $50,000 each by the smuggling ring.

–Tanya Weinbert,
Sun-Sentinel (Fort Lauderdale, Florida),
November 11, 2003

In its survey of 184 State and local police departments from across the United States, Abt Associates[24] asked how many had conducted investigations and made arrests for human traf ficking (which was among a list of transnational crimes they asked about). The sources of the trafficking were not delineated, but fewer than a third had conducted investigations, and fewer than a quarter had made arrests in any instances of human trafficking. Extrapolating from this to how much of their activity may have involved Asian organized crime, this would again seem to produce relatively small figures.

A review of recent Federal indictments involving all forms of Asian organized crime supports the point further. A request to the Organized Crime and Racketeering Section of the U.S. Department of Justice produced 11 Racketeer Influenced and Corrupt Organizations (RICO) indictments of Asian criminals for a variety of crimes in the United States. The indictments covered the period 1993 to 2002. (These were not all the cases involving Asian organized crime, nor a representative sample of all the cases. Instead, they are simply an opportunity sample.)

Seven of the eleven indictments charged crimes that could be construed to be related to human trafficking, e.g., interstate travel for illegal sexual activities, prostitution, kidnapping and hostage taking, asylum fraud, and alien smuggling. Perhaps the best known of these cases is the "Sister Ping" case. Chen Chui Ping, who is referred to as "the mother of all snake-heads," allegedly earned $30 million over 15 years transporting thousands of undocumented Chinese people into the United States. To do so, she retained subcontractors in New York and other United States cities. These included the notorious Fuk Ching gang in New York, who performed the domestic chore of transporting smuggled Chinese from Boston to New York City. Apart from this connection with a known criminal group, Sister Ping and her operation very much exemplify an entrepreneurial criminal network as opposed to a transnational organized crime group.

Keeping in mind the proviso about representativeness above, the first general observation that can be made is that seven such cases over a 10-year period again does not appear to be an especially large number. Secondly, an examination of the details in the indictments indicates that most of these cases involved crimes that were indeed organized by opportunistic networks, e.g., Sister Ping, and not by traditional and well-defined Asian organized crime groups having the characteristics outlined previously. This reinforces the earlier observation that it is the opportunistic, rather than the organized, crime groups who are the key players in Asian transnational crime.

That the transportation of human beings across borders is a smuggling rather than a trafficking issue, that it is conducted by entrepreneurial criminal networks rather than by traditional organized crime, and that the estimates of victims and cases may be overstated does not mean that there is no reason for concern. There are current estimates that some 11 million illegal immigrants are living in the United States. No one knows how many of these may be Asian. What can be assumed, however, is that any substantial number affects United States resources. Demands on education, health care, and social services and for jobs have a financial impact. This point is reflected in a study visit to a village near Fuzhou in China that has been the source of much smuggling of people to the United States. There, 35 to 40 Chinese children of preschool age were referred to by an official guide as "citizens," as in U.S. citizens. They were children born in the United States, now being raised in China until they reach school age, at which point they will return to the United States for schooling. The costs of educating these children—many of whom have parents who were illegal immigrants—will obviously have a financial impact on the United States.

Impact on Broader U.S. Interests

Irrespective of how much crime emanating from Asia may actually show up on United States shores, broader United States interests are at stake here. These interests relate to humanitarian concerns, to business interests, to political relationships, to investments in training and assistance, and to law enforcement cooperation.

The United States does, and very much should, have an interest in what happens to trafficking victims and to persons who are being smuggled across national borders. This interest exists apart from the question of how many such persons actually end up in the United States. It is a humanitarian and human rights issue. As elsewhere in the world, the problem in Asia requires effort and investment on both the demand and supply sides of the human trafficking/smuggling equation. Economic development and opportunity must be coupled with action to combat exploitative sex tourism, corruption, and official indifference.

U.S. business interests in Asia include casinos in Macau and trade in China and Taiwan. To the extent that the local and regional organized crime in these countries penetrates, interferes with, and jeopardizes business, it is harmful to U.S. interests. A specific example of this sort of harm is the crime of intellectual property theft, including software piracy. All six of the criminal organizations surveyed in Taiwan and Hong Kong, for example, are reported to be involved in pirated CDs and DVDs. In the case of the Wo Shing Wo, it is said to be the dominant activity in which the group is involved. A U.S. customs off icial interviewed in Beijing stressed the problem of intellectual property theft as a major concern.

As elsewhere, the United States has made a considerable investment in law enforcement training and assistance in Asia. The United States, for example, operates the International Law Enforcement Training Academy in Bangkok that has trained hundreds of law enforcement operatives from throughout the region. It is obviously in the best interests of the United States to see this investment pay off, which would lead to more effective combating of the crime problems described herein. With respect specif ically to drug trafficking, the DEA emphasized in the course of this study that China is a critically important player on the Asian drug scene; it was described as the key to heroin trafficking. What is needed, according to the DEA, is more joint investigative training and exchanges of intelligence information between the United States and China.

The United States must balance politically its interests in China, Hong Kong, and Taiwan. Because the crime problems covered by this study are, for the most part, regional problems, they require regional solutions. It is in the U.S. interest to play the role of honest broker in helping the region deal with organized crime.

Finally, a number of law enforcement officials, particularly in Taiwan and China, expressed dissatisfaction with Interpol and with cooperation from U.S. law enforcement. Interpol is regarded as basically ineffective. With respect to U.S. cooperation, the officials complained of essentially being ignored when they made requests for information and assistance. The Mutual Legal Assistance Treaty system was criticized as involving too much "red tape." Whatever the merits of these complaints, they obviously have implications for U.S. efforts to secure information and assistance for its own investigations.

CONCLUSION

The National Institute of Justice has recognized that crime and criminals more and more have a global face. This recognition means expanding NIJ's international research agenda to both better appreciate and to better understand potential threats from transnational crime. This preliminary assessment of Asian organized crime, including the pinpointing of potential research issues of mutual interest and the identification of potential research partners in Asia, lays a solid foundation for that expanded research agenda.

End Notes

[1] Gilboa, Amit, *Off the Rails in Phnom Penh: Into the Dark Heart of Guns, Girls, and Ganja*, Bangkok: Asia Books, 2001.

[2] He Bingsong, *Organized Crime in China, Beijing*: China Legal Press, 2002 (Chinese language publication).

[3] Smith, Paul, ed., *Human Smuggling*, Washington, DC: Center for Strategic and International Studies, 1997; Kwong, Peter, *Forbidden Workers*: *Illegal Chinese Immigrants and American Labor*, New York: The New Press, 1997; Emerton, Robyn, "Trafficking of Women Into Hong Kong for the Purpose of Prostitution: Preliminary Research Findings," Occasional Paper No. 3, Hong Kong: University of Hong Kong, 2001; Brazil, David, *No Money, No Honey!: A Candid Look at Sex-for-Sale in Singapore*, Singapore: Angsana Books, 2004.

[4] Chin, Ko-lin, *Smuggled Chinese: Clandestine Immigration to the United States*, Philadelphia: Temple University Press, 1999.

[5] Chu, Yiu-kong, *Triads as Business*, London: Routledge, 2000.

[6] Lo, T. Wing, *Corruption and Politics in Hong Kong and China*, Buckingham: Open University Press, 1993.

[7] Hill, Peter, *The Japanese Mafia: Yakuza, Law, and the State*, New York: Oxford University Press, 2003; Kaplan, David, and Alec Dubro, *Yakuza: Japan's Criminal Underworld*, Berkeley: University of California Press, 2003.

[8] Kaplan and Dubro, *Yakuza: Japan's Criminal Underworld* (see note 7).

[9] Santos, Aida, *Patterns, Profiles and Health Consequences of Sexual Exploitation: The Philippine Report*, Manila: Coalition Against Trafficking in Women, 2002.

[10] Chin, Ko-lin, *Heijin: Organized Crime, Business, and Politics in Taiwan*, Armonk, NY: M.E. Sharpe, 2003.

[11] Chang Tseng-liang, "A Study on the Problem of 'Fake Marriage' Across Taiwan Strait, Focusing on Fake Marriage for the Purpose of Prostitution," *Central Police University Journal of Police Science* 33 (1) (2002): 203–236 (Chinese language publication).

[12] Phongpaichit, Pasuk, and Sungsidh Piriyarangsan, *Corruption and Democracy in Thailand*, Chiang Mai: Silkworm Books, 1994.

[13] Asia Watch, *A Modern Form of Slavery: Trafficking of Burmese Women and Girls Into Brothels in Thailand*, New York: Human Rights Watch, 1993; Brown, Louise, *Sex Slaves: The Trafficking of Women in Asia*, London: Virago Press, 2000; Jeffrey, Leslie Ann, *Sex and Borders: Gender, National Identity, and Prostitution Policy in Thailand*, Chiang Mai: Silkworm Press, 2002.

[14] United Nations Centre for International Crime Prevention, "Overview of the 40 Criminal Groups Surveyed," *Trends in Organized Crime* 6 (2) (2000): 131–135.

[15] Chu, Yiu-kong, Triads as Business (see note 5); Hill, Peter, *The Japanese Mafia: Yakuza, Law, and the State* (see note 7); Zhang, Sheldon, and Ko-lin Chin, "The Declining Significance of Triad Societies in Transnational Illegal Activities," *British Journal of Criminology* 43 (3) (2003): 463–482.

[16] Zhang, Sheldon, and Ko-lin Chin, "Enter the Dragon: Inside Chinese Human Smuggling Operations," *Criminology* 40 (4) (November 2002): 737–768.

[17] Zhang and Chin, "The Declining Significance of Triad Societies in Transnational Illegal Activities," 463–482 (see note 15).

[18] Raymond, Janice, and Donna Hughes, "Sex Trafficking of Women in the United States," final report for the National Institute of Justice, grant number 98–WT–VX–0032, 2002, NCJ 187774.

[19] Estes, Richard, and Neil Weiner, "The Commercial Sexual Exploitation of Children in the U.S., Canada, and Mexico," final report for the National Institute of Justice, grant number 1999–IJ–CX–0030, 2002, NCJ 195561.

[20] Abt Associates, "Survey of Practitioners to Assess the Local Impact of Transnational Crime," final report for the National Institute of Justice, contract number 99–C–008 T005, Washington, DC, December 2003.

[21] Lintner, Bertil, Blood Brothers: *The Criminal Underworld of Asia*, New York: Palgrave McMillan, 2002.

[22] Raymond and Hughes, "Sex Trafficking of Women in the United States" (see note 18).

[23] Estes and Weiner, "The Commercial Sexual Exploitation of Children in the U.S., Canada and Mexico" (see note 19).

[24] Abt Associates, "Survey of Practitioners to Assess the Local Impact of Transnational Crime" (see note 20).

In: Organized Crime in the U.S.
Editor: Wesley B. Knowles

ISBN: 978-1-60741-524-4

Chapter 3

AFRICAN ORGANIZED CRIME

Federal Bureau of Investigation

AFRICAN CRIMINAL ENTERPRISES

African criminal enterprises have developed quickly since the 1980s due to the globalization of the world's economies and the great advances in communications technology. Easier international travel, expanded world trade, and financial transactions that cross national borders have enabled them to branch out of local and regional crime to target international victims and develop criminal networks within more prosperous countries and regions.

The political, social, and economic conditions in African countries like Nigeria, Ghana, and Liberia also have helped some enterprises expand globally.

African criminal enterprises have been identified in several major metropolitan areas in the U.S., but are most prevalent in Atlanta, Baltimore, Chicago, Dallas, Houston, Milwaukee, Newark, New York, and Washington, D.C.

Nigerian criminal enterprises are the most significant of these groups and operate in more than 80 other countries of the world. They are among the most aggressive and expansionist international criminal groups and are primarily engaged in drug trafficking and financial frauds.

The most profitable activity of the Nigerian groups is drug trafficking: delivering heroin from Southeast and Southwest Asian into Europe and the U.S. and cocaine from South America into Europe and South Africa. Large populations of ethnic Nigerians in India, Pakistan, and Thailand have given these enterprises direct access to 90 percent of the world's heroin production. The associated money laundering has helped establish Nigerian criminal enterprises on every populated continent of the world.

Nigerian groups are famous globally for their financial frauds, which cost the U.S. alone an estimated $1 billion to $2 billion each year. Schemes are diverse, targeting individuals, businesses, and government offices.

Here's just a partial list of their fraudulent activities: insurance fraud involving auto accidents; healthcare billing scams; life insurance schemes; bank, check, and credit card fraud; advance-fee schemes known as 4-1-9 letters; and document fraud to develop false identities. The advent of the Internet and e-mail have made their crimes more profitable and prevalent.

How We Combat African Criminal Enterprises

The FBI participates in two initiatives to bolster efforts to combat African criminal enterprises:

The Department of Justice Nigerian Crime Initiative coordinates the federal investigations of Nigerian criminal enterprises by using joint task forces in six major U.S. cities.

The Interpol West African Fraud annual conference brings together law enforcement agents from around the world to discuss and share information about the financial frauds perpetuated by criminal enterprises whose members are predominantly West African, and specifically Nigerian Criminal Enterprises.

In: Organized Crime in the U.S.
Editor: Wesley B. Knowles

ISBN: 978-1-60741-524-4

Chapter 4

ASIAN ORGANIZED CRIME

Federal Bureau of Investigation

ASIAN CRIMINAL ENTERPRISES

Asian criminal enterprises have been operating in the U.S. since the early 1900s. The first of these groups evolved from Chinese tongs—social organizations formed by early Chinese-American immigrants. A century later, the criminalized tongs are thriving and have been joined by similar organizations with ties to East and Southeast Asia.

Members of the most dominant Asian criminal enterprises affecting the U.S. have ties—either directly or culturally—to China, Korea, Japan, Thailand, the Philippines, Cambodia, Laos, and Vietnam. Other enterprises are emerging as threats, however, including groups from the South Pacific island nations.

These enterprises rely on extensive networks of national and international criminal associates that are fluid and extremely mobile. They adapt easily to the changes around them, have multilingual abilities, can be highly sophisticated in their criminal operations, and have extensive financial capabilities. Some enterprises have commercialized their criminal activities and can be considered business firms of various sizes, from small family-run operations to large corporations.

Asian criminal enterprises have prospered thanks largely to the globalization of the world economies and to communications technology and international travel. Generous immigration policies have provided many members of Asian criminal enterprises the ability to enter and live on every populated continent in the world today undetected.

There are two categories of Asian criminal enterprises. Traditional criminal enterprises include the Chinese triads (or underground societies) based in Hong Kong, Taiwan, and Macau as well as the Japanese Yakuza or Boryokudan. Non-traditional criminal enterprises include groups such as Chinese criminally influenced tongs, triad affiliates, and other ethnic Asian street gangs found in several countries with sizeable Asian communities.

Asian criminal enterprises conduct traditional racketeering activities normally associated with organized crime: extortion, murder, kidnaping, illegal gambling, prostitution, and loansharking. They also smuggle aliens, traffic heroin and methamphetamine; commit financial frauds; steal autos and computer chips; counterfeit computer and clothing products; and launder money.

There are several trends among Asian criminal enterprises. First, it is more common to see criminal groups cooperate across ethnic and racial heritage lines. Also, some gangs and criminal enterprises have begun to structure their groups in a hierarchical fashion to be more competitive, and the criminal activities they engage in have become globalized. Finally, more of these criminal enterprises are engaging in white-collar crimes and are co-mingling their illegal activities with legitimate business ventures.

In the U.S., Asian criminal enterprises have been identified in more than 50 metropolitan areas. They are more prevalent in Boston, Chicago, Honolulu, Las Vegas, Los Angeles, New Orleans, New York, Newark, Philadelphia, Portland, San Francisco, Seattle, and Washington, D.C.

How We Combat Asian Criminal Enterprises

The FBI participates in different working groups and initiatives to combat Asian organized crime on an international level:

The FBI/National Police Agency of Japan Working Group meets annually to discuss ongoing investigations and policy matters for sharing intelligence, interagency investigative support, and FBI extraterritorial operations in Japan.

Project Bridge is a working group under Interpol to help member countries coordinate investigations and information sharing between police agencies to fight Asian-alien smuggling syndicates.

The Interagency Working Group on Alien Smuggling coordinates policy discussions and examines investigative issues relating to alien smuggling and the trafficking of women and children. It is sponsored by the National Security Council's Special Coordination Group on International Crime.

The International Asian Organized Crime Conference meets annually, bringing together law enforcement agencies from around the world to discuss new trends and exchange ideas on combating Asian organized crime.

The Canadian/United States Cross-Border Crime Forum addresses cross-border crime issues and effective coordination between the U.S. and Canadian law enforcement.

The International Law Enforcement Academy in Bangkok, Thailand, is run with assistance from the FBI and Australian federal law enforcement agencies. The academy provides training to law enforcement agents from several Southeast Asian countries.

In: Organized Crime in the U.S.
Editor: Wesley B. Knowles
ISBN: 978-1-60741-524-4

Chapter 5

BALKAN ORGANIZED CRIME

Federal Bureau of Investigation

BALKAN ORGANIZED CRIME

The term "Balkan Organized Crime" applies to organized crime groups originating from or operating in Albania, Bosnia-Herzegovina, Croatia, Kosovo, the former Yugoslav Republic of Macedonia, Serbia and Montenegro, Bulgaria, Greece, and Romania. Balkan organized crime is an emerging threat in the U.S. While several groups are active in various cities across the country, they do not yet demonstrate the established criminal sophistication of traditional Eurasian or La Cosa Nostra (LCN) organizations. However, they have proven themselves capable of adapting to expanding criminal markets and becoming involved in new activities, much like the historical growth of other organized crime groups.

HISTORY OF BALKAN ORGANIZED CRIME

Organized crime in the Balkans has its roots in the traditional clan structures. In these largely rural countries, people organized into clans with large familial ties for protection and mutual assistance. Starting in the 15th century, clan relationships operated under the kanun, or code, which values loyalty and besa, or secrecy. Each clan established itself in specific territories and controlled all activities in that territory. Protection of activities and interests often led to violence between the clans. The elements inherent in the structure of the clans provided the perfect backbone for what is considered modern-day Balkan organized crime.

Many years of communist rule led to black market activities in the Balkans, but the impact of these activities was limited to the region. When communism collapsed in the late 1980s and early 1990s, it led to the expansion of Balkan organized crime activities. Criminal markets once closed to Balkan groups suddenly opened, and this led to the creation of an international network. Within the Balkans, organized crime groups infiltrated the new democratic institutions, further expanding their profit opportunities.

Balkan criminal organizations have been active in the U.S. since the mid-1980s. At first, these organizations were involved in low-level crimes, including bank robberies, ATM burglaries, and home invasions. Later, ethnic Albanians affiliated themselves with the established LCN families in New York, acting as low-level participants. As their communities and presence have become more established, they have expanded to lead and control their own organizations.

There is no single Balkan "Mafia," structured hierarchically like the traditional LCN. Rather, Balkan organized crime groups in this country translated their clan-like structure to the United States. They are not clearly defined or organized and are instead grouped around a central leader or leaders. Organized crime figures maintain ties back to the Balkan region and have established close-knit communities in many cities across the nation.

Albanian organized crime activities in the U.S. include gambling, money laundering, drug trafficking, human smuggling, extortion, violent witness intimidation, robbery, attempted murder, and murder. Balkan organized crime groups have recently expanded into more sophisticated crimes including real estate fraud.

In: Organized Crime in the U.S.
Editor: Wesley B. Knowles
ISBN: 978-1-60741-524-4

Chapter 6

EURASIAN ORGANIZED CRIME

Federal Bureau of Investigation

EURASIAN ORGANIZED CRIME

We apply the term "Eurasian Organized Crime" to organized crime groups comprised of criminals born in or with family from the former Soviet Union or Central Europe. These groups operate in numerous countries around the world, including the U.S., where their criminal activities cause hundreds of millions of dollars in losses to U.S. businesses, investors, and taxpayers through sophisticated fraud schemes and public corruption.

HISTORY OF EURASIAN ORGANIZED CRIME

The roots of Eurasian organized crime in the U.S. lie with the Vory V Zakone or "thieves in law," career criminals who banded together for support and profit in the Soviet prison system. During the Soviet period, their leaders or "shop managers" were illicitly paid a 30 percent margin to acquire scarce consumer goods and divert raw materials and finished goods from production lines for the benefit of Nomenklatura, or the educated elite, and criminals.

With the collapse of the Soviet Union in 1991, members allied themselves with corrupt public officials to acquire the control of industries and resources that were being privatized. This gave the syndicate a one-time infusion of wealth and supplied the infrastructure for continuing cash flows and opportunities to launder criminal proceeds. In February 1993, Boris Yeltsin, the first elected president of the Federation of Russian States, said, "Organized crime has become the No. 1 threat to Russia's strategic interests and to national security...Corrupted structures on the highest level have no interest in reform."

Organized crime members first emerged in the West in the 1970s when Soviet Refuseniks were allowed to emigrate to Europe, Israel, and the U.S. Among the Refuseniks were criminals who sought to exploit their new-found freedoms. These criminals helped the major criminal groups expand to the West when the Soviet Union collapsed and the people of the region were able to move about freely.

These groups based in the former Soviet Union have also defrauded newly formed governments of billions of dollars, as industries and resources formerly owned by the government have been privatized. They profit through tax-evasion schemes and using corrupt officials to embezzle government funds.

Their activity threatens to destabilize the emerging political institutions and economies of the former Soviet Union, where nuclear weapons remain deployed. The potential political and national security implications of this destabilization cannot be ignored. In the U.S., they are heavily involved in healthcare fraud, auto insurance fraud, securities and investment fraud, money laundering, drug trafficking, extortion, auto theft, and the interstate transportation of stolen property. They also are active in human smuggling and prostitution.

To concentrate on the activities of these organized crime groups, the FBI established investigative squads in New York and Los Angeles in 1994, San Francisco in 1995, Miami in 1997, Philadelphia in 1998, and in Newark and Chicago in 1999.

How We Combat Eurasian Organized Crime

The FBI belongs to several international working groups to combat the influence and reach of Eurasian Organized Crime and limit its impacts on all countries.

Eurasian Organized Crime Working Group

Acting under the auspices of the G8, this working group evolved from a group established in 1994. It meets to discuss and jointly address the transnational aspects of Eurasian organized crime that impact member countries and the international community in general. The member countries are Canada, Great Britain, Germany, France, Italy, Japan, the U.S., and Russia.

Central European Working Group

In 1995, our Eurasian Organized Crime Unit developed the concept and hosted the first meeting of the Central European Working Group at the International Law Enforcement Academy in Budapest, Hungary. Participants at the first meeting were law enforcement representatives from the Czech Republic, Slovakia, Hungary, Poland, Austria and Germany.

This group is part of a project that brings together the FBI and Central European law enforcement agencies to discuss cooperative investigative matters covering the broad spectrum of Eurasian organized crime. A principal concern is the growing presence of Russian and other Eurasian organized criminals in Central Europe and the U.S.

The initiative works on practical interaction between the participating agencies to establish lines of communication and working relationships, to develop strategies and tactics to address transnational organized crime matters impacting the region, and to identify potential common targets. Within a year, the working group had expanded to include law enforcement agencies and representatives from Romania, the Ukraine, Russia, Israel, Great Britain, and Belgium.

Southeast European Cooperative Initiative

The Southeast European Cooperative Initiative is an international organization intended to coordinate police and customs regional actions for preventing and combating trans-border crime. It is headquartered in Bucharest, Romania, and has 12 fully participating member countries. The U.S. has been one of 14 countries with observer status since 1998.

The initiative's center serves as a clearing house for information and intelligence sharing, allowing the quick exchange of information in a professional and trustworthy environment. The initiative also supports specialized task forces for countering trans-border crime such as the trafficking of people, drugs, and cars; smuggling; financial crimes; terrorism; and other serious trans-border crimes.

The 12 member countries are Albania, Bosnia and Herzegovina, Bulgaria, Croatia, Greece, Hungary, Macedonia, Moldova, Romania, Slovenia, Serbia/Montenegro, and Turkey. The observers are Austria, Azerbaijan, Belgium, Canada, France, Georgia, Germany, Italy, the Netherlands, Portugal, Spain, Ukraine, the United Kingdom, and the U.S.

In: Organized Crime in the U.S.
Editor: Wesley B. Knowles
ISBN: 978-1-60741-524-4

Chapter 7

ITALIAN ORGANIZED CRIME

Federal Bureau of Investigation

ITALIAN ORGANIZED CRIME—OVERVIEW

Since their appearance in the 1800s, the Italian criminal societies known as the Mafia have infiltrated the social and economic fabric of Italy and now impact the world. They are some of the most notorious and widespread of all criminal societies.

There are several groups currently active in the U.S.: the Sicilian Mafia; the Camorra or Neapolitan Mafia; the 'Ndrangheta or Calabrian Mafia; and the Sacra Corona Unita or United Sacred Crown.

We estimate the four groups have approximately 25,000 members total, with 250,000 affiliates worldwide. There are more than 3,000 members and affiliates in the U.S., scattered mostly throughout the major cities in the Northeast, the Midwest, California, and the South. Their largest presence centers around New York, southern New Jersey, and Philadelphia.

Their criminal activities are international with members and affiliates in Canada, South America, Australia, and parts of Europe. They are also known to collaborate with other international organized crime groups from all over the world, especially in drug trafficking.

The major threats to American society posed by these groups are drug trafficking and money laundering. They have been involved in heroin trafficking for decades. Two major investigations that targeted Italian organized crime drug trafficking in the 1980s are known as the "French Connection" and the "Pizza Connection."

These groups don't limit themselves to drug running, though. They're also involved in illegal gambling, political corruption, extortion, kidnapping, fraud, counterfeiting, infiltration of legitimate businesses, murders, bombings, and weapons trafficking. Industry experts in Italy estimate that their worldwide criminal activity is worth more than $100 billion annually.

A Long History

These enterprises evolved over the course of 3,000 years during numerous periods of invasion and exploitation by numerous conquering armies in Italy. Over the millennia, Sicilians became more clannish and began to rely on familial ties for safety, protection, justice, and survival.

An underground secret society formed initially as resistance fighters against the invaders and to exact frontier vigilante justice against oppression. A member was known as a "Man Of Honor," respected and admired because he protected his family and friends and kept silent even unto death.

Sicilians weren't concerned if the group profited from its actions because it came at the expense of the oppressive authorities. These secret societies eventually grew into the Mafia.

Since the 1900s, thousands of Italian organized crime figures—mostly Sicilian Mafiosi—have come illegally to this country. Many who fled here in the early 1920s helped establish what is known today as La Cosa Nostra or the American Mafia.

Charles "Lucky" Luciano, a Mafioso from Sicily, came to the U.S. during this era and is credited for making the American La Cosa Nostra what it is today. Luciano structured the La Cosa Nostra after the Sicilian Mafia. When Luciano was deported back to Italy in 1946 for operating a prostitution ring, he became a liaison between the Sicilian Mafia and La Cosa Nostra.

Sicilian Mafia (Based in Sicily)

The Sicilian Mafia formed in the mid-1800s to unify the Sicilian peasants against their enemies. In Sicily, the word Mafia tends to mean "manly." The Sicilian Mafia changed from a group of honorable Sicilian men to an organized criminal group in the 1920s.

In the 1950s, Sicily enjoyed a massive building boom. Taking advantage of the opportunity, the Sicilian Mafia gained control of the building contracts and made millions of dollars. Today, the Sicilian Mafia has evolved into an international organized crime group. Some experts estimate it is the second largest organization in Italy.

The Sicilian Mafia specializes in heroin trafficking, political corruption, and military arms trafficking—and is also known to engage in arson, frauds, counterfeiting, and other racketeering crimes. With an estimated 2,500 Sicilian Mafia affiliates it is the most powerful and most active Italian organized crime group in the U.S.

The Sicilian Mafia is infamous for its aggressive assaults on Italian law enforcement officials. In Sicily the term "Excellent Cadaver" is used to distinguish the assassination of prominent government officials from the common criminals and ordinary citizens killed by the Mafia. High-ranking victims include police commissioners, mayors, judges, police colonels and generals, and Parliament members.

On May 23, 1992, the Sicilian Mafia struck Italian law enforcement with a vengeance. At approximately 6 p.m., Italian Magistrate Giovanni Falcone, his wife, and three police body guards were killed by a massive bomb. Falcone was the director of Criminal Affairs in Rome. The bomb made a crater 30 feet in diameter in the road. The murders became known as the Capaci Massacre.

Less than two months later, on July 19, the Mafia struck Falcone's newly named replacement, Judge Paolo Borsellino in Palermo, Sicily. Borsellino and five bodyguards were killed outside the apartment of Borsellino's mother when a car packed with explosives was detonated by remote control.

Under Judge Falcone's tenure the FBI and Italian law enforcement established a close working relationship aimed at dismantling Italian organized crime groups operating in both countries. That relationship has intensified since then.

Camorra or Neapolitan Mafia (based in Naples)

The word "Camorra" means gang. The Camorra first appeared in the mid-1800s in Naples, Italy, as a prison gang. Once released, members formed clans in the cities and continued to grow in power. The Camorra has more than 100 clans and approximately 7,000 members, making it the largest of the Italian organized crime groups.

In the 1970s, the Sicilian Mafia convinced the Camorra to convert their cigarette smuggling routes into drug smuggling routes with the Sicilian Mafia's assistance. Not all Camorra leaders agreed, leading to the Camorra Wars that cost 400 lives. Opponents of drug trafficking lost the war.

The Camorra made a fortune in reconstruction after an earthquake ravaged the Campania region in 1980. Now it specializes in cigarette smuggling and receives payoffs from other criminal groups for any cigarette traffic through Italy. The Camorra is also involved in money laundering, extortion, alien smuggling, robbery, blackmail, kidnapping, political corruption, and counterfeiting.

It is believed that nearly 200 Camorra affiliates reside in this country, many of whom arrived during the Camorra Wars.

'Ndrangheta or Calabrian Mafia (Based in Calabria)

The word "'Ndrangheta" comes from the Greek meaning courage or loyalty. The 'Ndrangheta formed in the 1860s when a group of Sicilians was banished from the island by the Italian government. They settled in Calabria and formed small criminal groups.

There are about 160 'Ndrangheta cells with roughly 6,000 members. They specialize in kidnapping and political corruption, but also engage in drug trafficking, murder, bombings, counterfeiting, gambling, frauds, thefts, labor racketeering, loansharking, and alien smuggling.

Cells are loosely connected family groups based on blood relationships and marriages. In the U.S., there are an estimated 100-200 members and associates, primarily in New York and Florida.

Sacra Corona Unita or United Sacred Crown (Based in the Puglia Region)

Law enforcement became aware of the Sacra Corona Unita in the late 1980s. Like other groups, it started as a prison gang. As its members were released, they settled in the Puglia region in Italy and continued to grow and form links with other Mafia groups. The Sacra Corona Unita is headquartered in Brindisi, located in the southeastern region of Puglia.

The Sacra Corona Unita consists of about 50 clans with approximately 2,000 members and specializes in smuggling cigarettes, drugs, arms, and people. It is also involved in money laundering, extortion, and political corruption. The organization collects payoffs from other criminal groups for landing rights on the southeast coast of Italy, a natural gateway for smuggling to and from post-Communist countries like Croatia, Yugoslavia, and Albania.

Very few Sacra Corona Unita members have been identified in the U.S., although some individuals in Illinois, Florida, and New York have links to the organization.

La Cosa Nostra

La Cosa Nostra is the foremost organized criminal threat to American society. Literally translated into English it means "this thing of ours." It is a nationwide alliance of criminals—linked by blood ties or through conspiracy—dedicated to pursuing crime and protecting its members.

La Cosa Nostra, or the LCN as it is known by the FBI, consists of different "families" or groups that are generally arranged geographically and engaged in significant and organized racketeering activity. It is also known as the Mafia, a term used to describe other organized crime groups.

The LCN is most active in the New York metropolitan area, parts of New Jersey, Philadelphia, Detroit, Chicago, and New England. It has members in other major cities and is involved in international crimes.

History of La Cosa Nostra

Although La Cosa Nostra has its roots in Italian organized crime, it has been a separate organization for many years. Today, La Cosa Nostra cooperates in various criminal activities with different criminal groups that are headquartered in Italy.

Giuseppe Esposito was the first known Sicilian Mafia member to emigrate to the U.S. He and six other Sicilians fled to New York after murdering the chancellor and a vice chancellor of a Sicilian province and 11 wealthy landowners. He was arrested in New Orleans in 1881 and extradited to Italy.

New Orleans was also the site of the first major Mafia incident in this country. On October 15, 1890, New Orleans Police Superintendent David Hennessey was murdered execution-style. Hundreds of Sicilians were arrested, and 19 were eventually indicted for the murder. An acquittal generated rumors of widespread bribery and intimidated witnesses. Outraged citizens of New Orleans organized a lynch mob and killed 11 of the 19 defendants. Two were hanged, nine were shot, and the remaining eight escaped.

The American Mafia has evolved over the years as various gangs assumed—and lost—dominance over the years: the Black Hand gangs around 1900; the Five Points Gang in the 1910s and '20s in New York City; Al Capone's Syndicate in Chicago in the 1920s. By the end of the '20s, two primary factions had emerged, leading to a war for control of organized crime in New York City.

The murder of faction leader Joseph Masseria brought an end to the gang warfare, and the two groups united to form the organization now dubbed La Cosa Nostra. It was not a peaceful beginning: Salvatore Maranzano, the first leader of La Cosa Nostra, was murdered within six months.

Charles "Lucky" Luciano became the new leader. Maranzano had established the La Cosa Nostra code of conduct, set up the "family" divisions and structure, and established procedures for resolving disputes. Luciano set up the "Commission" to rule all La Cosa Nostra activities. The Commission included bosses from six or seven families.

Luciano was deported back to Italy in 1946 based on his conviction for operating a prostitution ring. There, he became a liaison between the Sicilian Mafia and La Cosa Nostra.

Other Historical Highlights

1951

A U.S. Senate committee led by Democrat Estes Kefauver of Tennessee determined that a "sinister criminal organization" known as the Mafia operated in this nation.

1957

The *New York State Police uncovered a meeting of major LCN figures* from around the country in the small upstate New York town of Apalachin. Many of the attendees were arrested. The event was the catalyst that changed the way law enforcement battles organized crime.

1963

Joseph Valachi became the first La Cosa Nostra member to provide a detailed looked inside the organization. Recruited by FBI agents, Valachi revealed to a U.S. Senate committee numerous secrets of the organization, including its name, structure, power bases, codes, swearing-in ceremony, and members of the organization.

Today, La Cosa Nostra is involved in a broad spectrum of illegal activities: murder, extortion, drug trafficking, corruption of public officials, gambling, infiltration of legitimate businesses, labor racketeering, loan sharking, prostitution, pornography, tax-fraud schemes, and stock manipulation schemes.

THE GENOVESE CRIME FAMILY

Named after legendary boss Vito Genovese, the Genovese crime family was once considered the most powerful organized crime family in the nation. Members and their numerous associates engaged in drug trafficking, murder, assault, gambling, extortion, loansharking, labor racketeering, money laundering, arson, gasoline bootlegging, and infiltration of legitimate businesses.

Genovese family members are also involved in stock market manipulation and other illegal frauds and schemes as evidenced by the recent FBI investigation code named "*Mobstocks*."

The Genovese crime family has its roots in the Italian criminal groups in New York controlled by Joseph Masseria in the 1920s. The family history is rife with murder, violence, and greed.

EARLY HISTORY—MASSERIA AND MARANZANO

Masseria sparked the so-called "Castellammarese War" in 1928 when he tried to gain control of organized crime across the country. The war ended in 1931 when Salvatore Maranzano conspired with Masseria's top soldier, Charles "Lucky" Luciano, to have Masseria killed. Maranzano emerged as the most powerful Mafia boss in the nation, setting up five separate criminal groups in New York and calling himself "Boss of Bosses."

Two of the most powerful La Cosa Nostra families—known today as the **Genovese** and **Gambino families**—emerged from Maranzano's restructuring efforts. Maranzano named Luciano the first boss of what would later be known as the Genovese family. Luciano showed his appreciation less than five months later by sending five men dressed as police officers to Maranzano's office to murder him.

Luciano, Costello, and Genovese

With Maranzano out of the way, Luciano become the most powerful Mafia boss in America and used his position to run La Cosa Nostra like a major corporation. He set up the LCN Commission, or ruling body, composed of seven bosses, and divided the different rackets among the families.

In 1936, Luciano was sentenced to 30 to 50 years in prison. Ten years later, he was released from prison and deported to Italy, never to return. When he was convicted, Frank Costello became acting boss because Genovese—then just an underboss—had fled to Italy to avoid a murder charge. His return to the states was cleared when a key witness against him was poisoned and the charges were dropped.

Costello led the family for approximately 20 years until May of 1957 when Genovese took control by sending soldier Vincent "the Chin" Gigante to murder him. Costello survived the attack but relinquished control of the family to Genovese. Attempted murder charges against Gigante were dismissed when Costello refused to identify him as the shooter.

In 1959, it was Genovese's turn to go to prison following a conviction of conspiracy to violate narcotics laws. He received a 15-year sentence but continued to run the family through his underlings from his prison cell in Atlanta, Georgia.

Valachi Sings—and Lombardo Leads

About this time, Joseph Valachi, a "made man," was sent to the same prison as Genovese on a narcotics conviction. Labeled an informer, Valachi survived three attempts on his life behind bars. Still in prison in 1962, he killed a man he thought Genovese had sent to kill him. He was sentenced to life for the murder.

The sentencing was a turning point for Valachi, who decided to cooperate with the U.S. government. On September 27, 1963, he appeared before the U.S. Senate Permanent Subcommittee on Investigations and testified that he was a member of a secret criminal society in the U.S. known as La Cosa Nostra.

In 1969, several years after Valachi began cooperating with the FBI, Vito Genovese died in his prison cell. By then the Genovese family was under the control of Philip "Benny Squint" Lombardo. Unlike the bosses before him, Lombardo preferred to rule behind his underboss. His first, Thomas Eboli, was murdered in 1972. Lombardo promoted Frank "Funzi" Tieri, and later Anthony "Fat Tony" Salerno as his front men.

Throughout the 1980s, the Genovese family hierarchy went through several changes. Tieri, recognized on the street as the Genovese family boss in the late 1970s, was convicted for operating a criminal organization through a pattern of racketeering that included murder and extortion.

Salerno then fronted as boss until he had stroke in 1981. In 1985, Salerno and the bosses of the other four New York families were convicted for operating a criminal enterprise—the LCN Commission. Lombardo, his two captains in prison and his health failing, turned full control of the Genovese family over to Gigante—the man who tried to kill Costello 30 years earlier.

FISH ON THE HOOK

In 1986, a second member turned against the Genovese family when Vincent "Fish" Cafaro, a soldier and right-hand-man to Anthony Salerno, decided to cooperate with the FBI and testify. According to Cafaro's sworn statement, Gigante ran the family from behind the scenes while pretending to be mentally ill. Cafaro said this behavior helped further insulate Gigante from authorities while he ran the Genovese family's criminal activities.

Gigante's odd behavior and mumbling while he walked around New York's East Village in a bathrobe earned him the nickname "the Odd Father." After an FBI investigation, Gigante was convicted of racketeering and murder conspiracy in December 1997 and sentenced to 12 years. Another FBI investigation led to his indictment on January 17, 2002, accusing him of continuing to run the Genovese family from prison. He pled guilty to obstruction of justice in 2003.

Gigante died in prison in December 2005 in the same federal hospital where Gambino family leader John Gotti had died in 2002.

The Pantheon Project and the Italian American Working Group

Over the years, FBI investigations have revealed how organized criminal groups have proliferated and impacted much of the world. Partnerships with foreign law enforcement agencies are essential to combat global organized crime groups.

The Pantheon Project was developed to improve cooperation between Italy and the U.S. in fighting Italian organized crime. Through the project, two FBI investigators are detailed to the headquarters of the Italian National Police, while the FBI hosts two Italian officers. The investigators work side-by-side with host agents and other law enforcement officials to help investigate the Sicilian mafia and La Cosa Nostra. They also work on Albanian organized crime.

Italian American Working Group

The FBI takes part in the Italian American Working Group, which meets every year. The group addresses organized crime, cyber crime, money laundering, international terrorism, illegal immigration, cooperating witnesses, drug smuggling, art theft, extradition matters, and cigarette smuggling. The U.S. and Italy take turns hosting the meetings.

Labor Racketeering

Labor racketeering is the domination, manipulation, and control of a labor movement in order to affect related businesses and industries. It can lead to the denial of workers' rights and inflicts an economic loss on the workers, business, industry, insurer, or consumer.

The historical involvement of La Cosa Nostra in labor racketeering has been thoroughly documented:

More than one-third of the 58 members arrested in 1957 at the Apalachin conference in New York listed their employment as "labor" or "labor-management relations."

Three major U.S. Senate investigations have documented La Cosa Nostra's involvement in labor racketeering. One of these, the McClellan

Committee, in the late-1950s, found systemic racketeering in both the International Brotherhood of Teamsters and the Hotel Employees and Restaurant Employees International Union.

In 1986, the President's Council on Organized Crime reported that five major unions—including the Teamsters and the Laborers International Union of North America—were dominated by organized crime.

In the early 1980s, former Gambino Family Boss Paul Castellano was overheard saying, "Our job is to run the unions."

Labor racketeering has become one of La Cosa Nostra's fundamental sources of profit, national power, and influence.

FBI investigations over the years have clearly demonstrated that labor racketeering costs the American public millions of dollars each year through increased labor costs that are eventually passed on to consumers.

Labor unions provide a rich source for organized criminal groups to exploit: their pension, welfare, and health funds. There are approximately 75,000 union locals in the U.S., and many of them maintain their own benefit funds. In the mid-1980s, the Teamsters controlled more than 1,000 funds with total assets of more than $9 billion.

Labor racketeers attempt to control health, welfare, and pension plans by offering "sweetheart" contracts, peaceful labor relations, and relaxed work rules to companies, or by rigging union elections.

Labor law violations occur primarily in large cities with both a strong industrial base and strong labor unions, like New York, Buffalo, Chicago, Cleveland, Detroit, and Philadelphia. These cities also have a large presence of organized crime figures.

We have several investigative techniques to root out labor law violations: electronic surveillance, undercover operations, confidential sources, and victim interviews. We also have numerous criminal and civil statutes to use at our disposal, primarily through the Racketeer Influenced and Corrupt Organization (RICO) Statute.

The civil provisions of the RICO statute have proven to be very powerful weapons, especially the consent decrees. They are often more productive because they attack the entire corrupt entity instead of imprisoning individuals, who can easily be replaced with other organized crime members or associates.

Consent decrees are most effective when there is long-term, systemic corruption at virtually every level of a labor union by criminal organizations. A civil RICO complaint and subsequent consent decree can restore democracy to a corrupt union by imposing civil remedies designed to eliminate such corruption and deter its re-emergence.

The Teamsters are the best example of how efficiently the civil RICO process can be used. For decades, the Teamsters has been substantially controlled by La Cosa Nostra. In recent years, four of eight Teamster presidents were indicted, yet the union continued to be controlled by organized crime elements. The government has been fairly successful at removing the extensive criminal influence from this 1.4 million-member union by using the civil process.

We work closely with the Office of Labor Racketeering in the Department of Labor and with the U.S. Attorneys' offices in investigating violations of labor law.

In: Organized Crime in the U.S.
Editor: Wesley B. Knowles
ISBN: 978-1-60741-524-4

Chapter 8

MIDDLE EASTERN ORGANIZED CRIME

Federal Bureau of Investigation

MIDDLE EASTERN CRIMINAL ENTERPRISES

Since the 9/11 terrorist attacks, we have taken a new look at the various threats originating in the Middle East and from Middle Eastern communities in the U.S. Contrary to a prevailing notion prior to 9/11, the FBI and law enforcement in general have come to recognize that some Middle Eastern criminal groups have no nexus to terror. Instead, these groups have the same goals as any traditional organized crime ring—to make money through illegal activities.

The groups have been active in the U.S. since the 1970s in areas with significant Middle Eastern or Southwest Asian populations. These organizations are typically loosely organized theft or financial fraud rings formed along familial or tribal lines. They typically use small storefronts as bases for criminal operations.

What kinds of crime schemes do these enterprises engage in? Many kinds: automobile theft, financial fraud, money laundering, interstate transportation of stolen property, smuggling, drug trafficking, document fraud, health care fraud, identity fraud, cigarette smuggling, and the theft and redistribution of infant formula. These enterprises rely on extensive networks of international criminal associates and can be highly sophisticated in their criminal operations. Organizations often engage in joint criminal ventures with one another.

In the U.S., Middle Eastern Criminal Enterprises are most prevalent in Illinois, Ohio, New Jersey, and New York. Internationally, they thrive in Afghanistan, Pakistan, Iran, Turkey, the United Arab Emirates, and Canada.

Middle Eastern Criminal Enterprises include criminals from Afghanistan, Algeria, Bahrain, Egypt, India, Iran, Iraq, Israel, Jordan, Kuwait, Lebanon, Libya, Morocco, Oman, Pakistan, Qatar, Saudi Arabia, Syria, Tunisia, Turkey, United Arab Emirates, and Yemen.

Chapter Sources

The following chapters have been previously published

Chapter 1. - This is an edited, reformatted and augmented version of a CRS Report # R40525 for Congress publication dated April 2009.

Chapter 2. - This is an edited, reformatted and augmented version of a U. S. Department of Justice publication dated January 2007.

Chapter 3. - This is an edited, reformatted and augmented version of a Federal Bureau of Investigation publication dated May 2009.

Chapter 4. - This is an edited, reformatted and augmented version of a Federal Bureau of Investigation publication dated May 2009.

Chapter 5. - This is an edited, reformatted and augmented version of a Federal Bureau of Investigation publication dated May 2009.

Chapter 6. - This is an edited, reformatted and augmented version of a Federal Bureau of Investigation publication dated May 2009.

Chapter 7. - This is an edited, reformatted and augmented version of a Federal Bureau of Investigation publication dated May 2009.

Chapter. 8 - This is an edited, reformatted and augmented version of a Federal Bureau of Investigation publication dated May 2009.

INDEX

B

C

N

O

P

Q

R

U

V